T0233915

User-Centered
Data Management

Synthesis Lectures on Data Management

Editor
M. Tamer Özsu, *University of Waterloo*

Synthesis Lectures on Data Management is edited by Tamer Özsu of the University of Waterloo. The series will publish 50- to 125 page publications on topics pertaining to data management. The scope will largely follow the purview of premier information and computer science conferences, such as ACM SIGMOD, VLDB, ICDE, PODS, ICDT, and ACM KDD. Potential topics include, but not are limited to: query languages, database system architectures, transaction management, data warehousing, XML and databases, data stream systems, wide scale data distribution, multimedia data management, data mining, and related subjects.

User-Centered Data Management
Tiziana Catarci, Alan Dix, Stephen Kimani, and Giuseppe Santucci
2010

Data Stream Management
Lukasz Golab and M. Tamer Özsu
2010

Access Control in Data Management Systems
Elena Ferrari
2010

An Introduction to Duplicate Detection
Felix Naumann and Melanie Herschel
2010

Privacy-Preserving Data Publishing: An Overview
Raymond Chi-Wing Wong and Ada Wai-Chee Fu
2010

Keyword Search in Databases
Jeffrey Xu Yu, Lu Qin, and Lijun Chang
2009

User-Centered Data Management

Tiziana Catarci, Alan Dix, Stephen Kimani, and Giuseppe Santucci

ISBN: 978-3-031-00710-1   paperback
ISBN: 978-3-031-01838-1   ebook

DOI 10.1007/978-3-031-01838-1

A Publication in the Springer series
SYNTHESIS LECTURES ON DATA MANAGEMENT

Lecture #6
Series Editor: M. Tamer Özsu, *University of Waterloo*
Series ISSN
Synthesis Lectures on Data Management
Print 2153-5418   Electronic 2153-5426

User-Centered Data Management

Tiziana Catarci
University of Rome, "La Sapienza," Italy

Alan Dix
Lancaster University, UK

Stephen Kimani
CSIRO ICT Centre, Australia

Giuseppe Santucci
University of Rome, "La Sapienza," Italy

SYNTHESIS LECTURES ON DATA MANAGEMENT #6

ABSTRACT

This lecture covers several core issues in user-centered data management, including how to design usable interfaces that suitably support database tasks, and relevant approaches to visual querying, information visualization, and visual data mining. Novel interaction paradigms, e.g., mobile and interfaces that go beyond the visual dimension, are also discussed.

KEYWORDS

usability, user-centered design, visual data access, information visualization, visual data mining, universal usability

Contents

Preface

This lecture was initially intended to cover relevant issues in database user interfaces, mainly query interfaces. However, very soon, we realized that providing friendly access to information is much more than just designing nice interfaces; rather, it has to do with designing interactive systems that suitably fit the users' tasks, and this can be achieved by following a user-centered approach to system design. Second, nowadays the data that users want to access do not reside only in traditional databases, they are mainly on the web (available or hidden – it does not matter). Third, users do not limit themselves to just extracting the data; instead, they want to manipulate them, analyze them, and make sense out of them. Thus, user-oriented systems should provide more functionality, in addition to querying. Finally, while visual interfaces and information visualization techniques are usually considered the most usable approaches, categories of users and/or contexts exist for which they are not appropriate, so other interactive paradigms need to be explored.

The content of this lecture derives from all the above considerations. Indeed, the lecture starts in Chapter 1 by discussing the importance of adopting a user-centered approach. Chapter 2 takes the reader to the early days, where we find the initial use of visual interfaces to support database tasks. Visual representation, interaction, and perception are discussed. In Chapter 3 the discussion moves on to shed more light on two concepts behind database querying. The focus here is on information visualization and visual data mining. The discussion, in Chapter 4 , then describes non-traditional interfaces that are relevant to databases. In particular, the chapter looks at web data and mobile interfaces. Chapter 5 describes interfaces that go beyond the visual dimension. In particular, it discusses accessibility and aural interfaces.

Tiziana Catarci, Alan Dix, Stephen Kimani, and Giuseppe Santucci
June 2010

CHAPTER 1

Why User-Centered

In data management, the needs of the underlying technology often appear most demanding: choosing appropriate data formats, schema, and perhaps, importing data from heterogeneous sources into consistent relational databases. At best, the user interface is an afterthought, and, at worst, users can be seen as an inconvenience, people who may enter incorrect or inconsistent data and, therefore, should be protected against.

It is also obvious that the data are really ultimately there for people to use or benefit from; in other words, it is the users not the data that are important. However, it is easy for this ultimate purpose of data to be overshadowed by the more immediate and unforgiving constraints of technology.

A user-centered approach puts people at the heart of design. This is not just about the aesthetics of the screens "putting a nice user interface on it," but it permeates every aspect of the design of a system. If even the lowest-level of data is structured badly, it is very hard to create usable systems on top of it, and 'bad' here does not mean in terms of some sort of internal consistency, but it is, more fundamentally about being fit for purpose or fit for ultimate use.

This focus on the users is at the heart of user-centered design, in general. To some extent, user-centered data management is simply an application of this focus on the users and can incorporate general techniques that can be found in standard textbooks in the area (Dix et al., 2004; Preece et al., 1994; Shneiderman et al., 2009) and international standards, principally ISO 9241 and ISO 13407.

The rest of this first chapter gives a short introduction to some of these general principles. Section 1.1 gives a short motivating example that demonstrate some of the pitfalls when systems are designed without a user-centered focus. Section 1.2 then discusses the process of applying user-centered design and Section 1.3 the general notion of 'usability.' Finally, Section 1.4 looks at the cost–benefit trade-off when applying user-centered design, how to decide when you have done enough work.

Although these general principles of user-centered design can be applied on a bespoke basis to particular applications, there are also special issues that arise when we consider the users of applications in data management and particular kinds of user interfaces. It is on this more specific area of *user-centered data management* that we focus in the remainder of this lecture.

1.1 AN EXAMPLE – WHAT CAN GO WRONG?

To see why this focus on the user is so important, let's consider an example the authors encounter repeatedly. We are academics on examination boards when student grades are being discussed. It is common to see a departmental spreadsheet or bespoke database being used as the primary reference, not the official university data system. Later, the university system is updated from the department one, but it is the local data that are deemed canonical, not the 'official' central one. Similar stories can be told in industrial and governmental settings.

What is going on in such cases?

Sometimes, this is a matter of local politics where individuals want to retain a sense of control. One could argue that they should not do this, but, of course, this is natural, and any information system design that ignores these personal and political realities will fail.

Sometimes, it is due to poor usability of the central university information system. For example, most of the time during the exam board some sort of summary list of grades is used. However, if a grade needs to be altered it is often not possible to edit this in the list view, but, instead, one has to drill into the student's individual record or even navigate out of the list view and into a single student view. This is, perhaps, the easiest kind of problem to fix with 'add on' solutions: new screens or different means to update.

Sometimes, there is an intrinsic problem with the data structures. For example, it is common to attempt to enter the marks for a course, only to find that the central system refuses to allow the marks of one of the students to be entered. This is because, for some reason, the student is not formally registered for the course on the system and the marks table in the database requires the registration record as an integrity condition. While this makes perfect sense when looking at the internal database or low level business logic, it then causes problems under real use when the world is not perfectly consistent. While this can be corrected, the paperwork often takes some time, during which the student's marks cannot be collated, and the mark-sheets that were being used to enter the data may even be misplaced.

Note that in this last case, the fundamental data structures have favored consistency over currency and, in so doing, work against the human systems within which they need to work. This is not a case where a user interface can be 'bolted on' to an existing data system; the human social and organizational needs must be considered at the data design stage. In real use, it is common for there to be 'inconsistent' cases, that is, for the data that arises in real life to, in some way, break rules or constraints that would hold of 'ideal' data. This often happens temporarily during updates, but it can be longer lasting when information in the system is partial or incomplete (the student is de facto taking the course; he/she is just, for some reason, not registered in the system). However, data design often focuses on ensuring a consistent internal representation, however, inconsistent with reality. Often, it is better to adopt a data design that allows inconsistency, but it is, in some way, highlighted or flagged as needing attention: let the marks be entered, and raise a 'to do' that indicates something needs to be fixed.

In some cases, user needs can be incorporated in generic data design heuristics (such as allowing but highlighting inconsistency above). In many cases, one needs a much more detailed understanding of the particular nature of the users of the system and the context in which it will be used.

1.2   THE PROCESS OF USER-CENTERED DESIGN

There are almost as many ways to pursue a user-centered design approach as there are practitioners. However, the process in ISO 13407 human-centered design process is a good place to start as it is best based on practice and since publication heavily influences practice.

ISI 13407 identifies four principle activities:

(a) *Understand and specify the context of use* – Who are the potential users? What is the environment in which the system will be used?

(b) Understand and specify the user and business requirements – What do we want the proposed system to do?

(c) *Design the product* – Create a design/prototype that meets the goals identified in (c), given the contextual constraints in (d).

(d) Evaluation of the design – Does the design that has been created in (c) actually work?

Sometimes (a) and (b) are lumped together under a general heading of 'understanding' 'requirements' or 'analysis,' although they differ in that (a) is principally about what will not change once a new system is created, whereas (b) is precisely about what is hoped will change. However, the distinction is always fluid, as Schon, D. (1991) has argued, it is often the most successful designers who question the problem formulation; the context itself may need to be changed.

These first stages will typically involve observing, interviewing, or meeting with real end users, although this can be difficult, especially for widely dispersed users such as 'any web user' or very busy users such as senior managers. When users include small children, there can be special difficulties both in understanding their point of view and also because of legal constraints (Markopoulos et al., 2008). However, for all types of users, there are two fundamental problems. The first is trying to understand people who are often very different from yourself as designer. The second is, perhaps, more subtle, which is understanding the things that you share with users; as so much of our knowledge is tacit, done without being aware of it, sometimes, it can be more difficult to understand those closest to you.

Many people suggest using some form of participatory design approach (Greenbaum and Kyng, 1991) where the end users are brought into the design process and invited to become, not just subjects to be studied by the designers, but, effectively, part of the design team or co-designers. Note that this helps to address the first of the problems above, the otherness of users, but the analyst/designer still needs to use expert facilitation in order to uncover users' tacit knowledge.

There are many methods used in the design phase, but most end in some sort of prototype, although this can vary from sketches of a proposed interface, to be shown to prospective users, to fully working software. The prototype is particularly important in order to evaluate the design with real users.

Alternatively, some form of expert evaluation is used where a usability expert uses some forms of checklist or heuristics to guide a structured analytic assessment of the design. This is often performed on a screen-by-screen (or on the web page-by-page) fashion, for example, by asking, whether it is clear what to do next from the current screen.

There are generic heuristics (see Box) which apply to most kinds of systems, but they were originally developed during the creation of desktop systems. However, there are also heuristics for more specific domains such as mobile interfaces (Bertini et al., 2009).

> 1. Visibility of system status
> 2. Match between system and the real world
> 3. User control and freedom
> 4. Consistency and standards
> 5. Error prevention
> 6. Recognition rather than recall
> 7. Flexibility and efficiency of use
> 8. Aesthetic and minimalist design
> 9. Help users recognize, diagnose, and recover from errors
> 10. Help and documentation
> Nielsen's Top 10 Usability Heuristics 1–9 from (Nielsen, J., 1994) all 10 in (Nielsen, J., 2005)

Perhaps, the most crucial thing is that these stages of analysis, design, and evaluation occur in a cycle. There are small cycles, for example, during design gap in understanding of the users context or goals may become apparent. Similarly, evaluation may show how the design fails to meet the user requirements. However, there is also a bigger cycle, where the process of evaluation highlights aspects of the context or requirements that were otherwise missed. This is particularly important when creating radically new systems. Users find it hard to envisage something dramatically different from the status quo, but when faced with a potential design, they are often able to articulate potential uses that had previously not been considered.

1.3   USABLE SYSTEMS

Usability is a complex term including everything from surface aesthetics to organizational fit. ISO 9241 defines usability in terms of three factors:

Effectiveness – The accuracy and completeness with which specified users can achieve specified goals in particular environments.

Efficiency – The resources expended in relation to the accuracy and completeness of goals achieved.

Satisfaction – The comfort and acceptability of the work system to its users and other people affected by the work system's use.

This is a rather dry, committee definition but basically addresses the following:

Effectiveness – Does it do the job?

Efficiency – How easily does it do the job?

Satisfaction – How enjoyable (or at least un-stressful) is it to do the job?

While this can be interpreted to apply at the level of workgroups or organisations, it is more common to look only at the user directly interacting with a system. However, it is important to keep one's focus more broadly on all stakeholders. The interface to a CRM (customer relationship management) system at a call center does not just affect the telephonist taking the call, but also the customer at the other end, even though the customer does not directly interact with the CRM system or even know that it exists.

For many years, the first two factors in the ISO standard, effectiveness and efficiency, were dominant in usability thinking – basically allowing people to work better. However, gradually, the last of these, namely satisfaction, has become more important for several reasons. First, is has been widely recognized in work situations that a happy worker is a more productive worker! Second, enjoyment may now be the primary objective as computer systems have spread out of the office and into the home and public places. Finally, as many systems are now delivered over the web, applications that were once shrink wrapped (e.g., Word Processing) are now delivered as services (e.g., Google docs); while a product is delivered once only with a single purchase decision, services have many decision points – it is easy to change services and more importantly to maintain the users' good will. As we shall see in Section 4.1, this shift to web delivery also includes many traditional data services.

This shift of concerns has lead to the notion of *user experience* as part of, or often subsuming, usability. Instead of seeing users merely as operators, their overall experience of using a product or service becomes a primary goal.

Of course, users are not all the same, and this has led to a focus on customizability and personalization, both for desktop applications and for those delivered over the web. Perhaps, most importantly, we are not all the same in terms of our physical, perceptual, and cognitive abilities. With an aging population, 'disability' of some kind or another will become the norm – ignoring those with reduced or different abilities may cut you off from a large segment of the population. However, it is not just good ethics and good for business that one should cater for a wide range of abilities; in many countries, accessibility legislation demands that usability really means usability for everyone. Cutting corners on usability can land you in court. In Section 5.1, we examine some of the implications of accessibility for data management.

1.4   COST-BENEFITS OF USABILITY

Focusing on users takes time, effort, and money; it can be hard to quantify benefits and hence to determine just how much effort is worth spending to make improvements (although one can make good estimates Bias and Mayhew, 2005). Given this, it may be tempting to either ignore it as an issue entirely or, alternatively, to obsessively attempt to iron out every slight difficulty.

However, in order to avoid the high cost of poor utilization and produce a successful system, usability must be made a priority. In the example at the beginning of this section, we saw that poor usability often means people maintain parallel information systems. Also, if it is difficult to enter pertinent information, they may simply not bother to do so. Even though the problems are with superficial usability, political and social context are fundamental to the design of the data structure; in all cases, when people in an organisation keep parallel systems, the centrally held 'official' organizational data becomes unreliable and inconsistent with reality. Paradoxically, the attempt in the database to maintain data integrity, in the narrow sense of being a self-consistent model, actually works against *real* integrity so that the data held begin to diverge from the things in the real world they are intended to represent.

However, things can be much worse. In 1992 the London Ambulance installed a new computer-aided dispatch; although it was intended to be a new sleek automated system, it became a potentially fatal disaster (Sommerville, I., 2004). As soon as it was deployed, it became clear that, rather than streamlining dispatch, delays increased, and a short while after deployment, the entire system collapsed leading to an emergency re-introduction of the old manual system. There were numerous failures but not the least amongst these was a failure to take into account the complex human and organizational factors involved in the dispatch process. Although there was some debate, no deaths were unambiguously attributed to the incident, this was only by good fortune. Poor usability can kill.

Happily, the costs of usability failure are not always so severe, and in practice, one must strike a balance between the efforts spent making a system more usable and the benefits of the improvements.

In fact, there are two stages to this. First, find potential problems or potential things to improve; second, decide whether it is worth implementing a solution. For the latter, it is possible, in principle, to do a simple cost–benefit trade-off. Figure 1.1 shows this with the severity of a usability problem on the left axis and the cost to fix on the bottom (focusing here on problems, a similar analysis applies to potential improvements).

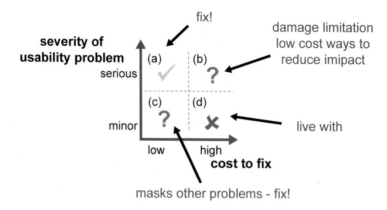

Figure 1.1: Cost-benefit trade-off for usability problems.

Easy cases are found at the top left and bottom right. In the first, (a) we have problems that are severe and have an easy and obvious fix, and, of course, one deals with these first. At the bottom right, (d) these are the minor problems that are hard to fix whereas, often, one must simply accept that they are there. An example of this might be a database configuration screen that is hard to understand. If configuration is only done occasionally and those doing it are highly trained, then we may simply assume they will read the documentation thoroughly on each occasion.

The cases at the top right and bottom left are where the decision on what action to take is more difficult even as the cost–benefit is more evenly balanced. On the bottom left (c) are minor problems that are easy to fix. Usually, it is worth dealing with these as they may mask other problems or generally reduce users' confidence in the system. However, they will, of course, have less priority than those at (a). Finally, at (b), there may be problems that have serious impact but are expected to be hard to fix. These are most problematic as some action is needed, but the costs of a 'proper' fix may be too high. In this case, the best option may be to seek workarounds that are not perfect but, in some way, limit or mitigate the problem.

One example of this last case (b) occurred in the online booking system of a large UK hotel chain. Web-based systems often have problems when users press 'back' in the middle of an interaction or use history, especially when viewing the confirmation page after completing a web form. In the case of this hotel, the effect was that the user could end up duplicating a booking. There are various ways this can be solved, but they often require a substantial re-engineering of the code. Instead of doing the 'proper' fix, they changed the system to simply refuse to create two identical bookings on the same day. This meant that if you did want to book two rooms in the same hotel, you needed to either do it as a single transaction, or wait a day for the second booking. However, this was a rare occurrence; the page that rejected the duplicate booking explained the cause, and it was a lot less damaging than accidentally repeated bookings.

Of course, the picture is somewhat simplistic. Severity is a multi-dimensional concept, which includes the likelihood of these particular problems: the number and kind of users who may encounter it (avoiding giving the CEO headaches) and the impact of the problem (death or minor inconvenience). The label 'cost to fix' also assumes one can assess this cost, and as in any area, this is a combination of experience and judgement. However, while these are not metric scales, it is still often not hard to rank issues against both these axes and so get some sense of the best place to focus effort.

Furthermore, this also assumes that we know what needs to be fixed. Finding problems is also a matter of the cost–benefit trade-off.

To find errors in a system, one of the most common ways is to try a prototype out with real users. This can be a costly business, both for the analyst doing the study and for the users who will need to stop doing their normal jobs while taking part in the study. Some years ago Nielsen and Landauer (1993) studied a number of large software projects in order to assess the optimal number of users to study in each iteration of a design. They found that there were diminishing returns in studying extra users, as many problems uncovered by a new user had already been uncovered by earlier users

– the exact proportions varied between projects, but often, they found that 70-80% of errors were uncovered by the first few users. Projects also differed in the costs of a re-design cycle during an iterative development cycle, and as a re-design could create fresh problems, it was not worth looking at too many users before doing redevelopment. The trade-off was different for each project, but on average, just five users was optimal, with a slightly higher figure for large complex projects and smaller for simpler ones. The figure of "five users is enough" is often taken a little too literally without looking at the specific context of Nielsen and Landaur's study, but the general lesson is that it is typically better to look at a relatively small number of users and fix the problems found thus far, before looking at more users.

As many systems are now deployed using web and agile methods in many projects, faster web-cycle times start to apply. The costs of performing modifications are usually quite low, with projects often having weekly or monthly update cycles. There is a temptation, especially with the web 2.0 philosophy of "perpetual beta," to simply release products and let the users act as test subjects. While sometimes developers do 'get away' with this kind of practice, it is clearly not the way to build customer confidence! However, these fast cycle times do change the cost–benefit trade-off, and given it is easier and faster to fix problems immediately, this should lead to a culture of continuous improvement of user experience rather than a big-bang approach during initial development.

CHAPTER 2

The Early Days: Visual Query Systems

Some of the earliest efforts to provide a user-centered approach to database management were the introduction of Visual Query Languages (VQLs). VQLs are languages for querying databases that use a visual representation to depict the domain of interest and express related requests. VQLs provide a language to express the queries in a visual format, and they are oriented towards a wide spectrum of users, especially novices who have limited computer expertise and who generally ignore the inner structure of the accessed database. Systems implementing VQLs are usually called Visual Query Systems (VQSs) (Catarci et al., 1997). In VQSs, the data representation language provides the user with a more natural view of the information, thus shortening the interpretation path that the user must perform to recognize the reality of interest from its computer-oriented representation. The same is true for the activity of expressing a query where direct manipulation of icons or navigation in diagrams substitute names of commands. Furthermore, visual languages are more flexible than traditional languages, where usually the learning of formal statements is needed to express even simple queries, each query being stated by a linear string where both operators and operands are expressed by words.

The advent of VQLs was due to several needs, including the following: providing a friendly human-computer interaction, allowing database search by non-technical users, and introducing a mechanism for comfortable navigation even in case of incomplete and ambiguous queries. It is worth noting that the real precursor of VQLs was Query-by-Example (QBE), proposed by Moshe Zloof in 1977 (Zloof, M., 1977). QBE was really ahead of its time. Indeed, Zloofs paper states: "the formulation of a transaction should capture the user's thought process…." This is a quite common idea today, but at that time (1977), the research on user interfaces and human-computer interaction was still in its infancy. It is worth noting that QBE is based not only on the usage of examples for expressing queries, but it also relies on the direct manipulation of relational tables inside a basic graphical user interface: an environment and an action modality that were quite unknown at that time. Another anticipatory idea is the incremental query formulation, i.e., "…the user can build up a query by augmenting it in a piecemeal fashion." Many current papers still recommend allowing the user to express the query in several steps, by composing and refining the initial formulations (Catarci et al., 1997). Finally, many of the QBE ideas are still up-to-date, and it is amazing to note that QBE-like interfaces are nowadays adopted in commercial database systems, despite the current explosion of sophisticated visualizations and interaction mechanisms.

VQSs received the greatest attention by the database community only later on, during the '80s and early '90s. The main distinguishing characteristic of VQSs with respect to traditional query environments is that they are user-oriented. As such, they should be tailored to help users in performing the tasks they have in mind. Therefore, the characteristics of the classes of users who will be working with a particular interface and the tasks such users need to perform have to be well understood. Since the purpose of VQSs is to provide access to the information contained in a database, the main user tasks are understanding the database content, focusing on meaningful items, finding query patterns, and reasoning on the query result. These tasks require specific techniques to be effectively accomplished, and such techniques involve activities such as pointing, browsing, filtering, and zooming that are typically provided by a visual interface.

VQSs can be classified according to two main criteria. The first one is the visual representation that the VQS adopts to present the reality of interest, the applicable language operators, and the query result. The query representation is generally dependent on the database representation since the way in which the query operands (i.e., data in the database) are presented constrains the query representation.

The second criterion for the proposed VQS classification refers to the (visual) interaction strategies provided to retrieve data. Data retrieval through interaction with a VQS is usually accomplished through the following two main activities:

- Understanding the reality of interest. The goal of this activity is the precise identification of the fragment of the schema the query refers to. Generally, the schema is much richer than the subset of concepts that are involved in the query. The result of this step is a query subschema, i.e., the static representation of all schema items that are needed to solve the query.

- Formulating the query. The query subschema can be manipulated in several ways, according to which query operators are provided. The goal of query formulation is to formally express the operations and operands that eventually make up the query.

2.1 VISUAL REPRESENTATION

The concept of 'representation' captures the fact that a sign stands in for, and takes the place of, something else (Mitchell, W., 1995). Visual representation, in particular, refers to the special case when these signs are visual (as opposed to textual, mathematical, etc.) (Tufte, E., 1983, 1990). Note that visual signs often represent non-visual objects and abstract concepts. Moreover, the term 'representation' is often overloaded and is used to imply the actual process of connecting the two realms of the original items and of their representatives.

The main purpose of adopting a visual representation in a query system is to clearly communicate to the user the information content of the database(s), concentrating on essential features, and omitting unnecessary details. Such information is internally structured in several way that mainly depend on the data model characteristics, but it must be rendered at the interface level in such a way that any user can easily grasp it. However, the interface visual representation has to be mapped in terms of internal database concepts in order to be dealt with by the system. To come up with this dual nature, a visual representation has to be based on a so-called *visual formalism*, a term introduced by David Harel as follows (Harel, D., 1988): "The intricate nature of a variety of computer-related systems and situations can, and in our opinion should, be represented via visual formalisms; visual because they are to be generated, comprehended, and communicated by humans; and formal, because they are to be manipulated, maintained, and analyzed by computers." Visual formalisms include familiar objects such as tables, diagrams, icons, etc.

In a VQS, the visual representation should effectively convey all and only the database information. In other words, a visual representation should be "consistent" with respect to the database it represents. We say that a representation is consistent if it is "correct and complete" (Haber et al., 1994). A visual representation is complete if the user can get from it all the database information, and it is correct if no other information can be derived from it. Note that using a consistent visual representation to depict the information of interest is crucial in order for the user to correctly grasp the database information content (see Mackinlay's pioneering work on automatic design of graphical presentations (Mackinlay, J., 1986) and a more recent book (Card et al., 1999) for many examples of misleading visual representations).

For example, let us consider the data in Table 2.1, which refer to towns in Italy, number of people living in each town, their location with respect to Rome and their distance in kilometers also with respect to Rome. We may visualize these data through a graph, as the one in Figure 2.1.

Town	People	# Position	Distance
Rome	4,000,000		0
Milan	1,800,000	North	600
Naples	1,500,000	South-East	200
Pisa	150,000	North-West	350
Pescara	200,000	East	220

Table 2.1: Example of database (Note, position relative to Rome).

In this case, the visualization is neither complete nor correct. It is not complete because not all attribute values in Table 2.1 have an appropriate representation. There is nothing in the figure to infer information about the approximate number of people, distance from Rome, or their mutual position. Moreover, the distribution of the towns in the graph may even convey wrong information about their position since Naples is very likely to be interpreted as being North of Rome, Milan as being East, etc., thus the visual representation is also not correct. The example in Figure 2.2 shows another graph, from which the user can infer all data in Table 2.1. This representation is complete and correct. Since we are referring to geographical information, we are taking into account that the observer usually considers the distribution of data on the plane according to the four cardinal points. There is a large amount of literature on this topic, starting from (Mackinlay, J., 1986) up to a variety of other

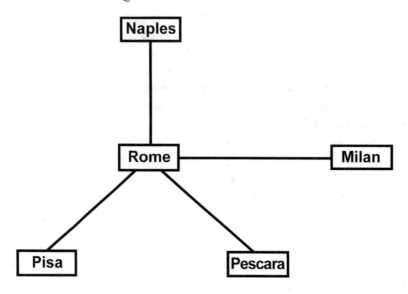

Figure 2.1: Visual representation of data in Table 2.1 which is neither complete nor correct.

projects, including the ZOO project at the University of Wisconsin (Haber et al., 1994), and many others. Typical limitations of many approaches are the lack of formal checking of the representation correctness and the visualization of either the schema or the instances of the database (not both). Moreover, some proposals are restricted to specific domains and/or applications instead of providing a general solution. The *DARE: Drawing Adequate REpresentations* project (Catarci and Santucci, 2001; Catarci et al., 2003) aims at overcoming the above limitations by 1) proposing a general theory for establishing the adequacy of a visual representation, once the database characteristics have been specified and 2) developing a system which implements such a theory and works in two modalities, namely:

Representation Check – Checking the adequacy of visual representations proposed by the user. The adequacy is expressed in terms of completeness and correctness of a visual representation with respect to a database.

Representation Generation – Automatically associating with any database the most effective visual representation. Such a visual representation has to be not only adequate (as mentioned above), but it also has to convey some database features specified by the designer (e.g., that some concepts are the most relevant).

Note that all mentioned approaches only deal with static representations and do not consider changes to the representation caused by the user interaction with the database or the appropriateness of such changes to reflect the user intentions and tasks (see Bizer et al., 2009; Cruz, James, and Brown, 1999; Catarci et al., 2007 for contributions on this aspect). The DARE

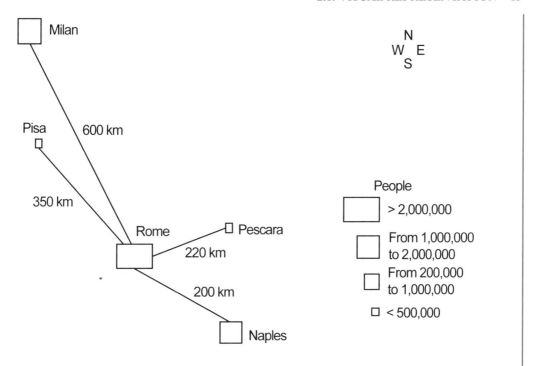

Figure 2.2: Correct and complete representation of data in Table 2.1.

system is based on a knowledge base containing different kinds of rules: 1) visual rules that char-
acterize the different kinds of visual symbols that are associated with the different kinds of visual
symbols; 2) data rules that specify the characteristics of the data model, the database schema, and
the database instances; 3) mapping rules that specify the link between data and visual elements (e.g.,
entities are represented as rectangles, Person is a red rectangle, John is a small red rectangle); and
4) perceptual rules that describe how the user perceives a visual symbol (i.e., a line, a geometric
figure, an icon, etc.), relationships between symbols (i.e., the mutual placements of two figures on
the plane), and what the perceptual effects are of relevant visual attributes such as color, texture, etc.

Associating an effective visual representation to any large data set is crucial to allow different
kinds of non-technical users to easily grasp the database information content. However, as opposed
to the case of data models, the creation suitable visual models is not straightforward, and it is still
an open problem how to do this, in general.

Despite the theory that aims to provide a correct and complete visual representation, existing
VQSs implement much more specific visual representations.

Form-based representations are the simplest way to provide users with friendly interfaces for
data manipulation. They are very common as application or system interfaces to relational databases
where the forms are actually a visualization of the tables. In query formulation, prototypical forms are

visualized for users to state the query by filling appropriate fields. In systems such as QBE (Zloof, M., 1977), only the intensional part of relations is shown: the user fills the extensional part to provide an example of the requested result. The system retrieves whatever matches the example. In more recent form-based representations, the user can manipulate both the intensional and the extensional part of the database.

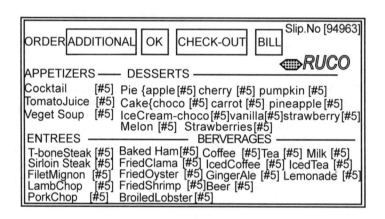

Figure 2.3: Example of early form-based representation in EMBS (based on Shirota et al., 1989).

Diagrammatic representations are widely used in existing systems. Typically, diagrams represent data structures displayed using visual elements that correspond to the various types of concepts available in the underlying data model.

Iconic representations use icons to denote both the objects of the database and the operations to be performed on them. A query is expressed primarily by combining operand and operator icons. In order to be effective, the proposed set of icons should be easily and intuitively understandable by most people. The need for users to memorize the semantics of the icons makes the approach manageable only for somehow limited sets of icons.

The **hybrid** representation is a combination of the above representations. Often, diagrams are used to describe the database schema, while icons are used either to represent specific prototypical objects or to indicate actions to be performed. Forms are mainly used for displaying the query result.

All of the above representations present complementary advantages and disadvantages. In early VQSs, only one type of representation was available to the user while more modern approaches aim at supporting interfaces offering different interaction representations and interaction modalities.

As in most graphical user interfaces, many VQSs have mainly stressed the user input aspects of the interaction and have given little thought to the visualization of output data. The results are usually presented by means of structured text, without considering other possible display formats. Conversely, an appropriate visualization of the query result allows the user to better capture the relationships amongst the output data.

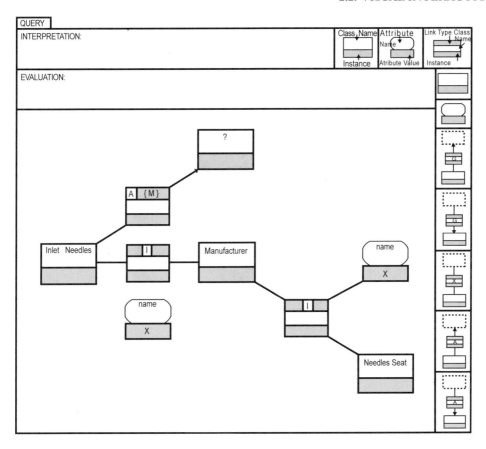

Figure 2.4: Example of diagrammatic representation (based on Mohan and Kashyap, 1993).

2.2   VISUAL INTERACTION

Visual Interaction refers to the kind of dialogue that users have with an interactive system that makes use of visual elements and strategies exploiting visual clues and perception. In traditional VQSs, visual interaction strategies are used to accomplish the two activities that make up data retrieval, i.e., understanding the reality of interest and formulating the query. In more recent systems, visual interaction also refers to the user's direct manipulation of the data display provided by the system. Note that some VQSs allow more than one strategy for each activity.

Understanding the reality of interest may be a complex task when the database schema is made of hundreds or thousands of concepts and/or the extension of the database is made of millions or billions of instances. What is needed is a mechanism to filter the information that is considered significant by the user. This may be achieved by means of a **top-down strategy**, where general aspects

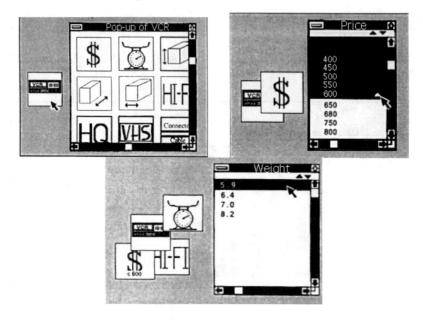

Figure 2.5: Example of iconic representation (from Tsuda et al., 1990).

of the reality are first perceived, and then specific details may be viewed. The top-down strategy is implemented in several ways. The first one can be seen as a sequence of iterative refinements, i.e., the system provides for each schema a library of top-down refinements. Each refinement can be obtained from the previous one by means of transformations, which, when applied to atomic objects, result in more detailed structures. A similar approach is implemented by providing either selective or hierarchical zoom. The user can also graphically edit the schema, so that irrelevant objects can be removed from the screen.

Another well established technique for learning about the information content of a schema is **browsing**. Browsing is essentially a viewing technique aimed at gaining knowledge about the database. In principle, it can handle both schemas and instances in a homogeneous way. Assuming that the user has only minor knowledge about the database, she/he starts the interaction by examining a concept and its neighborhood (adjacent concepts, i.e., concepts that are at distance one from the selected concept, can be considered as a first level of explanation of the examined concept). Next, a new element is selected by the user from adjacent concepts to be the current one, and its neighborhood is also shown: this process proceeds iteratively.

An alternative approach to top-down refinement and browsing is **schema simplification**. The idea here is to "bring the schema close to the query." This is done by building a user view resulting from aggregations and transformations of concepts of the original schema. While in the top-down approach, it is possible to locate concepts that exactly match the initial schema (at different levels of abstraction), in the schema simplification approach, the user may build a proper view of the original schema which cannot be extracted by the schema itself at any of its levels of abstraction.

Query formulation is the fundamental activity in the process of data retrieval. The query strategy by schema navigation has the characteristic of concentrating on a concept (or a group of concepts) and moving from it in order to reach other concepts of interest, on which further query predicates may be specified. Such a strategy differs according to the type of path followed during the navigation (see Figure 2.6 for an example of unconnected path).

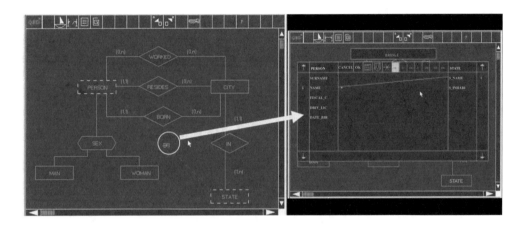

Figure 2.6: Unconnected path in QBD* (from Angelaccio et al., 1990).

A second strategy for query formulation is **by subqueries**. In this case, the query is formulated by composing partial results. The third strategy for query formulation is **by matching**. This is based on the idea of presenting the structure of a possible answer that is matched against the stored data.

The last strategy for query formulation is **by range selection**, allowing a search conditioned by a given range on multi-key data sets to be performed. The query is formulated through direct manipulation of graphical widgets, such as buttons, sliders, and scrollable lists, with one widget being used for every key. An interesting implementation of such a technique is *dynamic query* (Ahlberg and Shneiderman, 1994). The user can either indicate a range of numerical values (with a range slider) or a sequence of names alphabetically ordered (with an alpha slider). Given a query, a new query is easily formulated by moving the position of a slider with a mouse: this is supposed to give a sense of power but also of fun to the user, who is challenged to try other queries and see how the result is modified. Usually, input and output data are of the same type and may even coincide. Overall, visual interaction is based on the visual perception capabilities of the user.

2.3   VISUAL PERCEPTION

Visual perception is the ability to transform light stimuli reaching the eyes into information that can be recognized and processed. Perception is unavoidably selective: we can't see all there is to see. There are of course physiological limits (both for the human species and for individuals); some argue that there are limits to cognitive capacity. And then, there are the constraints of our locational viewpoint: we can't see things from every angle at once. But in addition to such physical limits, we focus on salient features and ignore details that are irrelevant to our current purposes or interests. Selectivity thus involves omission. People may either 'filter out' data or 'seek out' data of a certain kind.

Selective attention often involves redundancy: we don't always need much data in order to recognize something. Often, we can manage with minimal visual data, making use of what is called 'redundancy.' You may know those 'blocky' pictures of famous people in which you can just about recognize who it is. Our schemata allow us to 'fill in gaps' because we know what should be there. Objects, events or situations are 'sized up' in relation to our frames of reference, and these influence how perception is structured (Newcomb, T., 1952). Selective perception is based on what seems to 'stand out.' Much of this 'standing out' is related to our purposes, interests, expectations, past experiences and the current demands of the situation.

The characteristics of visual perception are exploited in visual systems in general and VQSs in particular. Indeed, they use visual representations based on visual signs (Bertin, J., 1981). Visual signs are characterized by a high number of sensory variables: size, intensity, texture, shape, orientation, and color. By exploiting the multi-dimensionality of visual representations, users are allowed to perform, in a single instant, a visual selection. Other constructions, for example a linear text, do not permit this immediate grasping since the entire set of correspondences may be reconstructed only in the user's memory. However, visual signs need to be used in an appropriate manner to avoid the user to derive from the visual representation incorrect information, i.e., information that is not actually stored in the data source, as discussed in Section 2.1 above. Moreover, the visual perception principles provide the scientific basis for the design of visual interfaces that best match the users requirements and effectively help them to make sense out of data.

CHAPTER 3

Beyond Querying

So far, we have concentrated mainly on user-oriented mechanisms to extract the information of interest from data sources. In this section, we see how visual mechanisms can be exploited to analyze and make sense out of the data.

3.1 INFORMATION VISUALIZATION

The fact that suitable visualizations could convey information in a quick and efficient way has been understood for a long time, and drawings and visualizations have been extensively used in different data analysis or information exchange contexts, e.g., teaching, designing, information spreading, data exploring, etc.

Among several, noticeable examples can be found the famous Dr. John Snow intuition of plotting deaths of cholera on a 1845 map of the Soho district of London and the pioneering approach of Harry Beck that proposed on 1931 a distorted map of the London underground.

The Snow's drawing (see Figure 3.1) allowed for visually identifying a concentration of deaths around the Broad Street water pump; closing that source of contaminated water resulted in a decrease in the number of deaths from cholera (Tufte, E., 1997).

The Beck's map, presenting the sequence of stations and their interchanges in a schematic and clearer way (disregarding a strict correlation with the real topography of the underground), is now influencing the maps of most transport systems throughout the world (see Figure 3.2).

Even if, in principle, as the two above examples testify, visualization has nothing to do with computers and paper based drawings could be very effective (and they still are), the modern interpretation of Information Visualization gives a central role to computational means, allowing quick data manipulation and highly interactive visualizations.

The basic visualization flow is depicted in Figure 3.3.

Data are 1) gathered from one or more data sources, 2) associated with a suitable *representation* that is then 3) *presented* to the end user who can manipulate it, changing some visualization parameters (e.g., point of view, or colors). More complex interaction paradigms do exist, allowing for presenting the users with multiple, correlated visualizations and providing means to visually select new data subsets, interacting with the available visualizations; the discussion of such kinds of interaction is out of the scope of this chapter.

It is worth noting that the steps followed by the paper based examples discussed so far are conceptually the same as the computer based visualizations: the designer has to manually extract relevant data from a data source (e.g., locations of cholera deaths), devise a suitable visual represen-

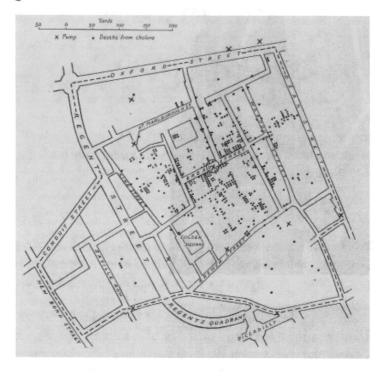

Figure 3.1: The Snow's drawing.

tation of that data (e.g., plotting deaths in the location in which they happened), and present it to the end user (e.g., producing a drawing like the one on Figure 3.3).

However, these steps are inherently static and do not easily scale to different data sets, representations, or presentations; conversely, the availability of a computer that allows for interactive data manipulation and transformation introduces new possibilities and new challenges. As an example, assume that Dr. Snow's target analysis covered the whole of London. In such a case, it is almost impossible to have a hand-drawing of the whole city, but it is a task that is trivial using a computer. On the other hand, how to *present* such a large map on a computer screen? Usual pan and zoom facilities are not enough, and new strategies are required.

As a more complex example, assume that we want to use colors to visualize, for each death, the closest pump. The calculation associated with this new *representation* is time consuming for a human-based drawing but can be easily implemented in a computer-based visualization. Moreover, it is worth noting that this information was not present in the original data, and it is a nice example of the kinds of *elaboration* that can produce better visualizations.

The above considerations lead to focus on three main issues: data extraction and elaboration, data representation, and data presentation, discussed in the following subsection.

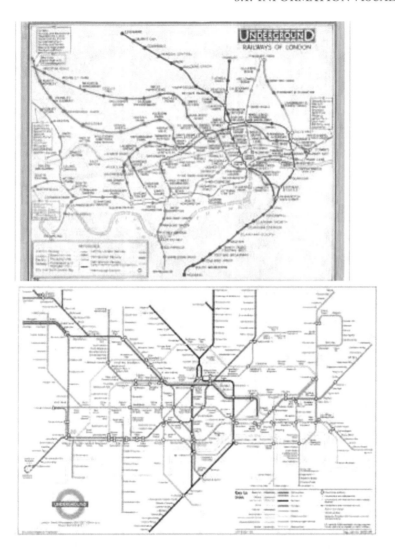

Figure 3.2: Original London's underground map. The Beck's distorted map.

3.1.1   DATA EXTRACTION AND ELABORATION

Most of the problems that confront an analyst while manipulating the data she wants to analyse come from the fact that data are often distributed, inconsistent, and present high dimensionality; in the following we detail these aspects.

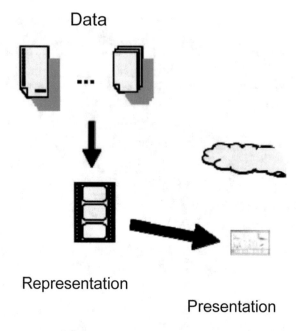

Figure 3.3: The visualization flow.

Distributed and Inconsistent Data

In a number of Information Visualization (Infovis) applications, it is necessary to integrate and query data coming from different heterogeneous data sources. This is inherently difficult (and not especially well researched), and is clearly a challenging activity. Moreover, this data comes in a variety of types and with different structures: including numeric and non-numeric data, images, videos, and models. To analyze all this in an integrated fashion is again a challenging activity.

The integration of heterogeneous data is a core activity in database research, and its importance and topicality are still increasing. However, it is mandatory to understand its role in the context of Infovis applications. Logic based systems (e.g., Calvanese et al., 2009), balancing expressive power and computational cost, represent the state-of-the-art solutions in data integration, and Infovis can greatly benefit from such an approach.

The main idea is to evaluate queries through a logic based engine that exploits a conceptual view of the application domain (i.e., an ontology), rather than a flat description of the data sources. Such a description, called global schema, is independent of the sources that are mapped through a logic language into concepts of the global schema. A robust and promising solution is to use description logics that are a fragment of the first order logic and balance expressive power and computational cost.

Data Quality

Databases often deal with data coming from multiple sources of varying quality: data could be incomplete, inconsistent, or riddled with measurement errors. To date, several research lines and commercial solutions have been proposed to deal with these issues in order to improve data quality.

Data inconsistencies have been initially studied by statisticians who needed to resolve discrepancies arising from large statistical surveys. One of the first analyzed problems was the presence of duplicate records of a person (Elmagarmid et al., 2007; Naumann and Herschel, 2010), and the devised practical and theoretical solutions, called record linkage, allow for obtaining and linking all the related data records, producing a unique and consistent view of that person. It was quickly understood that record linkage was only one of a larger set of problems, such as wrong, missing, inaccurate, and contradicting data, and in the late 1980's, researchers started to investigate all problems related to data quality. This was essentially pushed by both the increasing number of scientific applications based on large, numerical data sets and by the need to integrate data from heterogeneous sources for business decision making.

The problem of missing data was initially studied in the context of scientific/numerical data sets, relying on curative methods and algorithms able to rescue or normalize missing or wrong scientific/numerical data; more recently, the focus moved to non-numerical data, in order to improve also non-scientific data, improving exploratory queries, data integration, or the management of inherently not high quality data sets, like information extraction from web and sensor network applications; in addition, research activities are attempting to build general purpose uncertain data management systems, (e.g., Boulos et al., 2005).

Considering complementary goals, in order to ensure an overall data quality, the so called "data cleaning" activity has been investigated, i.e., the process of standardizing data representation and eliminating a wider range of errors. Data cleaning activities are about record matching and deduplication (i.e., recognizing that two or more retrieved data elements correspond to the same real world entity), about data standardization (i.e., adjusting data format and units), and about data profiling (i.e., evaluating the data quality), gathering several aggregate data statistics that constitute the data profile and ensuring that the values match up with expectations.

However, Infovis applications look at these issues in a different way, and the straightforward adoption of the solutions proposed in the database field could be either a valid solution or represent an obstacle to the analysis process. As an example, assume that we are dealing with a missing or erroneous value. The database techniques foresee some curative algorithms, providing an alternative (e.g., interpolated or statistically computed) value for the bad data, but this solution can hide an insight: as an example, it is possible that the fact the data are missing is an insight itself, e.g., you have discovered the wrong sensor or a person omitting a form field to evade a tax.

Multidimensional Data

Very often an Infovis application is about high dimensional data that are hard to present to the end user. Available techniques rely either on intrinsically high dimensional visualizations, e.g., parallel coordinates or scatterplot matrices (described in the next section) or on variations of basic data dimension reduction techniques, e.g., self organizing map (Kohonem, T., 2001), principal component analysis (Eick, S., 2000), and multidimensional scaling (Cox and Cox, 1994). The main idea is either to select a subset of the original dimensions that best represent some data feature (e.g., clustering) or to compute new, synthetic dimensions. However, it is not always clear which technique is better to use according to the data structure and task goals, and the relationship between the original data and the reduced data may be not intuitive. A comprehensive summary of data reduction techniques can be found in (Barbar et al., 1997).

When the data allow for arranging attributes through hierarchies, it is possible to reuse some results that come from OLAP (on-line analytical processing) applications. The term OLAP (Codd et al., 1993) refers to end-user applications for interactive exploration of large multidimensional data sets. OLAP applications rely on a multidimensional data model thought to explore the data from different points of view through the so called data cubes (or data hypercubes), i.e., measures arranged through a set of descriptive categories, called *dimensions* (e.g., sales for city, department, and week). Hierarchies are defined on dimensions, (e.g., week .. month .. year) to enable additional aggregation levels. A data cube may hold millions of entries, characterized by tens of dimensions, and the challenges come from the study of mechanisms able to insure interactivity, e.g., precomputing and storing different levels of the hierarchies to speed up the interaction, reducing in different ways the size of the data (see the next subsection), sacrificing precision for speed, and from the usability of the system: to gain insights into such huge and complex data, it is needed to project the hypercube onto bi-dimensional or three-dimensional spaces, thus requiring long and sometime frustrating explorations. Such approaches can be usefully adopted for reducing data dimensionality in Infovis applications.

Summarizing, the phase of data extraction and elaboration, while often neglected in Infovis applications or Infovis textbooks, is a crucial step that could strongly influence the quality of the overall visualization process.

3.1.2 DATA REPRESENTATION

Data representation corresponds to encoding data values and data relationships on an internal visual structure. In this phase, the designer is not concerned with the real screen size and capabilities; she has at her disposal, in principle, a perfect space with no dimension or resolution limitation; mapping such an ideal space on the final device is the goal of the presentation phase.

Most of the Infovis research in the last decades focused on designing suitable representations according to data characteristics, user tasks, and user perceptive and cognitive capabilities. Here we report the main results, considering the most common situation, and focusing on univariate, bivariate, and multivariate data (i.e., the number of attributes that the visual representation has to encode).

The simplest case we can consider is the encoding of single value, e.g., the temperature of an engine or the altitude of a plane. Even if this activity seems quite straightforward, some problems can arise in particular situations. A good example comes from the traditional aircraft altimeters, whose goal was uniquely to show the altitude in feet (see Figure 3.4), in which tree hands represent tens of thousand of feet (the smallest one), thousands of feet (the largest one), and hundreds of feet (the longest one). Under pressure and because of the pilot's continuous gaze movements, a visual effect can happen, the so called *change blindness*: a person viewing a visual scene fails to detect large changes in the scene during some visual disruption such as a saccade (eye movement). Assume that

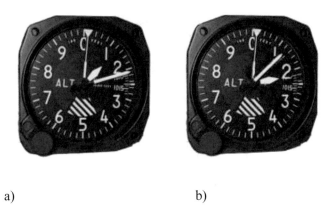

a)   b)

Figure 3.4: Two altimeters representing a) 1210 feet and b) 2100 feet.

the aircraft rises to 2100 feet while the pilot is controlling the speed; the altimeter moves from left situation to the right one. A quick look to the altimeter, in which hundred and thousand hands are switched, can result in the pilot failing to notice the difference.

Modern, digital altimeters follow the idea of representing univariate data along an axis, e.g., y-axis in the example shown in Figure 3.5. Some variation can exist on this representation, like using different scale distortion (e.g., log scale) or duplicating the information: in the example of Figure 3.5, the actual high is represented by both the cursor position and by the white digits over the black background; moreover, the "18" is emphasized, according to the pilots' culture: a pilot thinks in terms of hundreds of feet.

Other techniques do exist: continuously, varying values could be represented using a sequence of colors (pseudocoloring, see Ware, C., 2000); however, it is mandatory to consider some perceptual issues that can heavily affect the representation effectiveness: e.g., to convey the feeling of increasing values a good choice is to adopt a sequence of colors in which each color is lighter then the previous one (see, e.g., the color scale on Figure 3.6).

In most cases, however, the analysis is not about a single univariate value but about a collection of different data. Several, agreed solutions do exist, most of them sharing the need to scale to large data sets. One common solution is to plot values across an axis, using a pixel for each data value. As an example, Figure 3.7 (a) shows 2553 books, plotted along the x-axis according to their page number. Note that the range between 30 and 1000 pages is very crowded, and several collisions

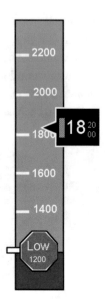

Figure 3.5: A modern altimeter encoding a single value across a linear axis (Redrawn from Spence, R., 2007).

Figure 3.6: A color scale in which each color is lighter then the previous one.

happen: it will be up to the presentation phase to deal with such an issue. On the other hand, some *aggregation* operation can assist the visual analysis: Figure 3.7 (b) shows the frequency distribution of the books' page numbers and Figure 3.7 (c) shows a box plot (Tukey, J., 1977) of the same data.

Likely, the most used representation of bivariate data is the scatterplot. Figure 3.8 shows the books of Figure 3.7 plotted by publication year (*y*-axis) and number of pages (*x*-axis). A quick glance reveals that the bigger books (more than 1000 pages) have been published after 1990, and that few books are older than 1976. In some domains, like medical, climate studies, or market analysis, one of the two attributes is the time, and the other one is a value that changes over time; in such cases, typical time series diagrams are used (see Figure 3.9). However, when the observed time ranges over cyclic periods (e.g., the hours of several consecutive days), some interesting alternatives do exist, allowing for easily comparing the periodicity of some behaviour. As an example, Figure 3.10 (a) shows a company network traffic among several days. Each concentric circle represents a day, while

a)

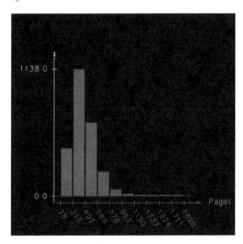

b)

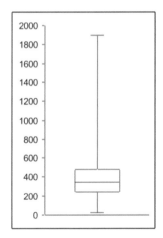

c)

Figure 3.7: (a) The page number values of 2553 books.
(b) The page number values of 2553 books.
(c) The page number values of 2553 books.

sectors refer to hour intervals in the day. In the picture, it is quite easy to discover a repetitive (and suspicious?) pattern of traffic (top left) few minutes before 22 pm. Figure 3.10 (b) represents the ozone level above Los Angeles over ten years. It is quite evident that the ozone level is higher during summer and that the values have decreased with time.

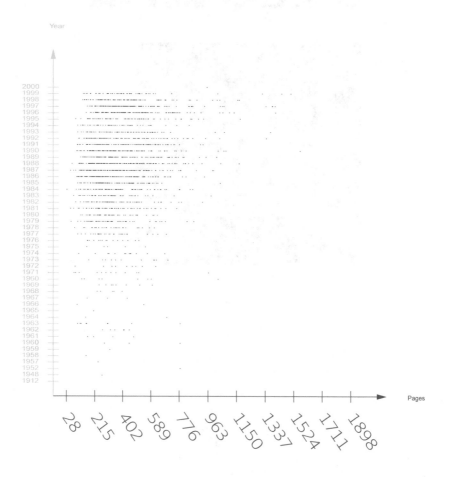

Figure 3.8: Plotting books according to page numbers and publication year.

Multivariate data are more complex to represent, considering "simple" trivariate data for which the intuitive idea of plotting points on three-dimensional scatterplots does not work well, for occlusion and perspective issues. As an example, consider the three-dimensional scatterplot on Figure 3.11 (a), plotting books using page numbers (x-axis), publication year (y-axis), and publisher (z-axis). What is the number of pages of the book in the red circle? Obviously, the answer could come from some interaction mechanisms, like changing point of view or adding some markers (see

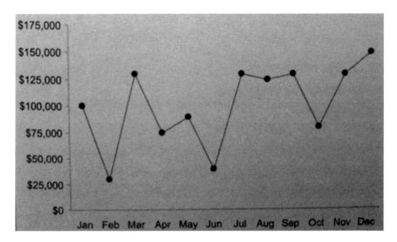

Figure 3.9: A time series describing the sales of a company across one year.

Figure 3.11 (b)). However, these issues belong to the presentation step and reduce somehow the presentation effectiveness.

Moreover, if we consider more than three attributes we have to devise, in any case, new strategies.

Four solutions are commonly available: reducing the dataset cardinality, encoding data attributes through additional visual attributes (e.g., size, color, shape, pattern, etc.), presenting the dataset through several, low-dimensional, views, and using representation mechanisms able to handle a large number of attributes.

The first strategy has been already analyzed in the previous section; here we discuss the last three ones.

Using more visual attributes makes possible to encode, in a two or three-dimensional scatterplot, up to 7 or 8 attributes. As an example, Figure 3.12 shows 6 books attributes: page number, publication year, and publisher are associated with x, y, and z axes, the color encodes the book's quality: red = good books, blue = bad books (according to Amazon), the size encodes the price (the bigger the more expensive), the shape encodes the language (sphere = Italian, pyramid = English). It is possible to use textures and orientations, reaching 8 attributes, but it is quite obvious that we are pushing the limits of this strategy: size and shape make occlusion problems more serious, and the representation becomes quickly unusable.

Colors can be used instead of shapes for labelling nominal scales; however, perceptual studies (Ware, C., 2000) show that it is hard to effectively distinguish more than ten colors, and, as a consequence, this approach does not scale to high cardinality nominal scales.

Parallel coordinates (Inselberg and Dimsdale, 1985) allow for handling, virtually, an infinite number of attributes. The space is represented through parallel lines, one for each attribute, and

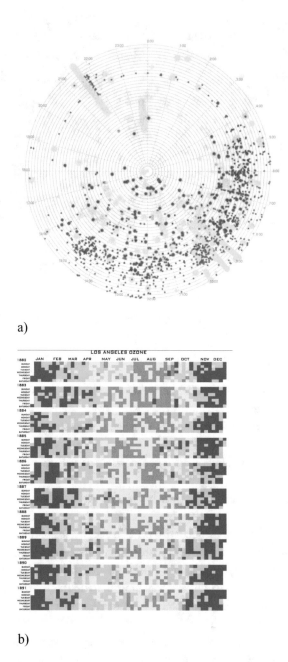

a)

b)

Figure 3.10: Representation of cyclic events (Redrawn from Spence, R., 2007).

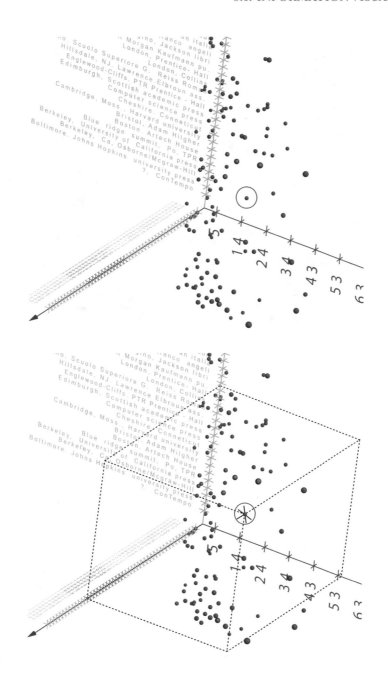

Figure 3.11: Perspective problems with three-dimensional scatterplots.

Figure 3.12: Representing up to 8 attributes in a three-dimensional scatterplot.

each data item is represented through a poly-line. Figure 3.13 shows a car dataset with 7 attributes (miles per gallon, number of cylinders, horsepower, weight, acceleration, year, and origin). Some data structures are quite evident: a high number of cylinders corresponds to low miles per gallon; however, the order of the coordinates strongly affects this visual relationship that is very clear, only if miles per gallon and number of cylinder axes are adjacent. This example puts into evidence one of the potential drawbacks of parallel coordinates: a wrong order of the axes could destroy the representation effectiveness.

A scatterplot matrix allows for exploring all the pairs of attributes of a multidimensional dataset, projecting them on bidimensional scatterplots that are arranged in a matrix. Figure 3.14 shows the scatterplot matrix for the wine dataset, a chemical analysis of 13 constituents of wines grown in a region of Italy. The matrix contains all the possible bidimensional scatterplots, and it is possible to explore all the potential attribute correlations. As an example, it is easy to see that attributes g and f (6th column, 7th row) present a strong correlation (points on the scatterplot are plotted along the bisector). On the other hand, the number of bidimensional scatterplots is $n \cdot (n - 1)/2$ (where n is the number of attributes), and for high-dimensional datasets, this approach forces the user to explore a very large number of scatterplots. In such a case, the presentation activity should assist the user in locating the most interesting projections.

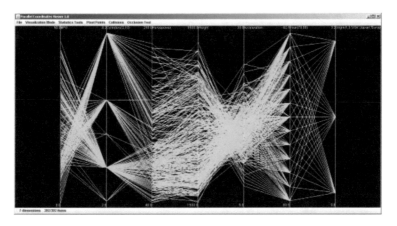

Figure 3.13: A parallel coordinates example.

3.1.3   DATA PRESENTATION

The best data representation could be totally useless if poorly *presented* to the end user. The main issues to consider in this phase are user interaction and space limitation.

User interaction deals with a set of very often neglected techniques that allow for basic, interactive manipulation of the visualization. A minimum list of interactions should include the following features:

- Panning, zooming, scrolling, and rotating capabilities;

- Axes reordering, e.g., exchanging the X axis with the Y axis;

- Axes' scales manipulation (e.g., logarithmic vs. linear) and labelling;

- Change of the association between data values and visualization;

- Single item inspection through direct manipulation, e.g., selecting it with a mouse;

- Interactive visual and textual data filtering, i.e., reducing the data presented on the screen;

- Saving and restoring of queries and visualizations;

- Simple mechanisms for data import/export;

- Undo and redo;

- Navigation support, i.e., providing clues for understanding how to move within the visualization;

- Animation.

Figure 3.14: The wine dataset scatterplot matrix.

It is the authors' belief that most of the available Infovis systems fail to address, in some way, these basic issues, resulting in systems that do not allow exploitation of all the underlying representation alternatives.

Space limitation refers to the problem of presenting the abstract representation on a real screen, taking into account screen size, collisions, user perception, etc. Several techniques have been developed to deal with such issues, and we discuss here the guidelines underlying them, providing some examples of their application.

It is possible to classify the available strategies into two main classes: the first one foresees drawing strategies that allow for mapping the representation onto the screen (e.g., providing zoom and pan mechanism), while the second one encompasses several algorithmic techniques that either try to ameliorate the image thereby reducing the clutter (e.g., sampling the dataset) or providing guidance to the end user to easily locate the most interesting visualizations (e.g., automatically selecting within a large scatterplot matrix the three most representative bi-dimensional scatterplots).

The devised strategies must scale to large datasets: as an example, consider the simple strategy of mapping a large image on the screen using zooming and scrolling; this can quickly result in boring, confusing, and time consuming activities. As an example, let us consider the editing of a very long document (i.e., thousand of pages) that requires only scrolling along the y-axis. Without some additional techniques, it becomes very hard to locate a specific page or to understand the part of the document one is looking for. If we switch to a very large two-dimensional map, used by a user who needs to explore only the details on a few parts of the map (e.g., the start street and the arrival street of a long trip), the situation is even worse; it requires changing the zoom level during the interaction and to scroll the image on both axes.

An effective solution for dealing with this problem is to arrange the presentation in such a way that it always presents the user with an overview as well as the details in the representation, clearly visualizing the relationships that exist among these two views. This technique is called either *focus plus context* or *overview plus detail*. In Figure 3.15, two examples are presented, one for browsing a map (a) and another for a Word document (b).

A second strategy, which still allows for presenting the whole image in an effective way is called *distortion*. The idea is to enlarge, in some way, only *a part* of the image, providing details in that part and leaving the overall image available for providing an overview. In Figure 3.16, we see two examples of such a technique. In table lens (Rao and Card, 1994), depicted in Figure 3.16 (a), the representation is a simple Excel spreadsheet in which numerical values are coded through bars, and it is possible to enlarge one or more rows to read the figures underlying the bars. The perspective wall (Mackinlay et al., 1991) allows for browsing a large horizontal figure that is distorted on three planes, getting details on the central part and preserving the overall perception of the image. In Figure 3.16 (b), this technique is used to browse a file system where rows represent types of documents and columns the creation date.

Semantic zoom is a technique that removes/resumes details from an image according to the level of zoom. A very known example comes from Google Earth in which, for example, city names appear only when the zoom factor is above a specific threshold. Semantic zoom can be usefully combined with pan for preserving the overview. In Figure 3.17, an example from Google Earth is shown: while panning from New York to Rome, Google Earth performs a semantic zoom that allows the end user to retain an overview of the whole transformation.

Problems may arise while visualizing large data sets, very likely producing cluttered images, and they have been thoroughly analyzed by the Infovis community and a survey can be found in (Ellis and Dix, 2007). Decluttering techniques are classified in three groups: appearance, spatial distortion, and temporal. Appearance includes techniques affecting the presentation look: point size, altering opacity and color, and sampling and filtering. Spatial distortion encompasses point or line displacement, topological distortion stretching the presentation, either non-uniformly (e.g., Fisheye) or uniformly (e.g., zoom), representing data items as single pixel, space filling, and dimensional reordering. Animation techniques use the time axis to reduce clutter. As an example, Figure 3.18 (b) shows the result of a non-uniform sampling technique (Bertini and Santucci, 2006) able to rescue density differences in a crowded Figure 3.18 (a) bidimensional scatterplot (postal parcels plotted by weight and volume).

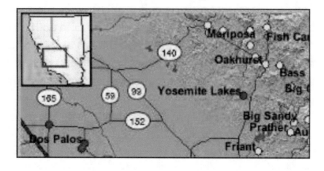

(a)

(b)

Figure 3.15: Focus plus context examples.

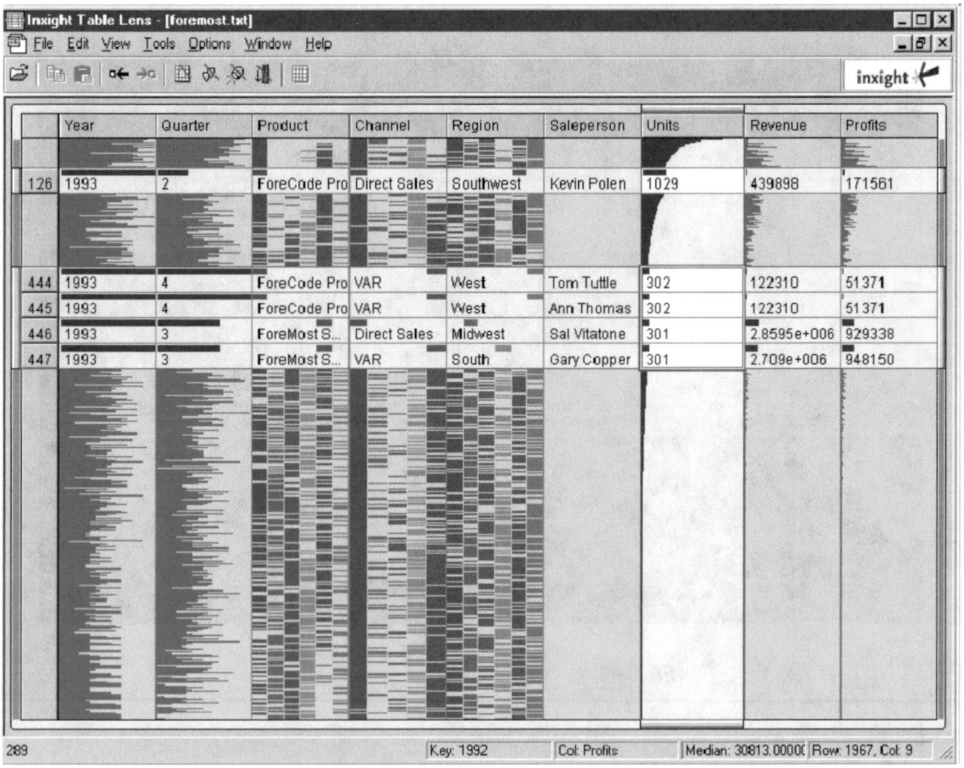

Figure 3.16: Examples of distortion.

A similar objective has been pursued by other researchers whose main goal is to find the best mapping between the dataset and specific visual configurations. Scagnostics is a graph theoretic technique (Tukey, J., 1977; Wilkinson et al., 2005) in which the idea is to compute a series of measures on a scatter plot matrix (see the example in Figure 3.14), which maps all the data dimensions in a series of two-dimensional scatter plots to select pairs of dimensions showing the most interesting patterns. A similar approach (Schneidewind et al., 2006) uses the same basic framework but is extended to include pixel-based visualizations.

3.2   VISUAL DATA MINING

This part of the chapter sheds light on various aspects pertinent to another technique to make sense out of data – visual data mining.

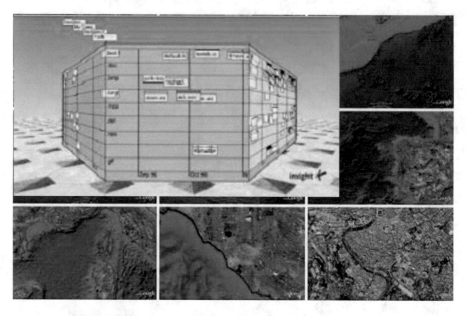

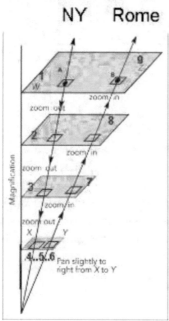

Figure 3.17: Semantic zoom and panning from New York to Rome.

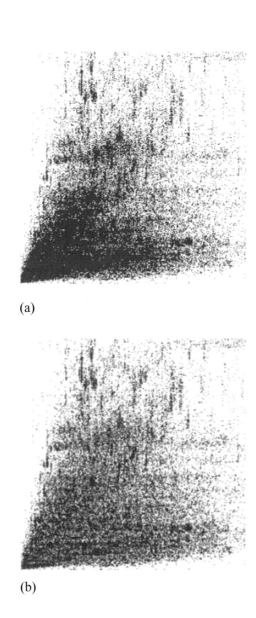

(a)

(b)

Figure 3.18: Non uniform sampling.

3.2.1 BACKGROUND

There are several fields that are core to visual data mining, including the following: information visualization, knowledge discovery, and data mining. Information visualization has been introduced in the previous subsection. In the sequel, we introduce knowledge discovery and data mining.

Knowledge Discovery

Knowledge discovery (KD) may be defined as the process of identifying valid, novel, potentially useful, and ultimately understandable models and/or patterns in data (Fayyad et al., 1996a,b). On the whole, the knowledge discovery process may be defined as an interactive and iterative non-trivial process that entails various phases as seen in Figure 3.19.

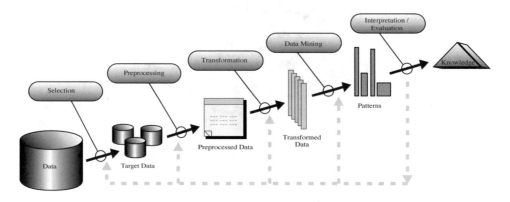

Figure 3.19: The Knowledge Discovery process (based on Fayyad et al., 1996a).

The KD phases include the following: carrying out some initial planning (understanding the application domain, relevant prior knowledge, and goal(s) of the user), data integration, selection of target data, data cleaning and pre-processing, data reduction and transformation, selection of suitable data mining techniques to support the discovery process, and evaluation, presentation and interpretation of results. Through carrying out the phases, the KD process intends to find a subset of results that may be considered as new "knowledge" (Fayyad et al., 1996a,b). KD is of interest to researchers in many research disciplines such as the following: machine learning, pattern recognition, databases, statistics, artificial intelligence, expert systems, and information visualization.

Data Mining

Data mining is a step in the knowledge discovery process that, under acceptable computational efficiency limitations, enumerates models and patterns over the data (Fayyad et al., 1996a,b). Data mining methods include the following: clustering, classification, regression, characterization, dependency modeling change and deviation detection, and pattern-based similarity matching.

The primary goals of data mining are verification and discovery. The verification goal aims at validating some hypotheses based on specific user needs. The user generates a series of hypothetical patterns and relationships (assumptions or claims). The user then formulates and issues queries to the system (actually, to the data itself), and to verify (or disprove) the claims. The discovery goal involves finding "new" patterns or discovering new knowledge. Rather than verify hypothetical patterns, the goal here is to use the data to uncover or identify such patterns. Such methods of discovery may be initiated based on the guidance of a user to analyze a certain domain through a predetermined perspective or by automated learning. Discovery can be predictive or descriptive. Prediction entails "foretelling" unknown or future values of the same variables or other variables of interest whereas description involves getting an interpretation/understanding of the data. Classification, regression and time series models are primarily useful for prediction. Clustering, association and sequence discovery models are primarily useful for description of the behavior that is captured in the data.

3.2.2   DEFINITION AND IMPORTANCE OF VISUAL DATA MINING

In the KD or data mining process, only the user can ultimately or directly determine the usefulness or value of some resulting knowledge in a specific domain or application. On the same note, different users may rate the same knowledge very differently. What one user considers valuable may be deemed to be of less or no value by another user (Ankerst, M., 2001). The human user is potentially resourceful and instrumental in guiding or steering the entire discovery process. Human involvement in the KD process is pivotal in the mining and acquisition of useful knowledge. Moreover, the human-vision channel has outstanding capabilities that enable both recognition and understanding of overwhelming data in an instant (Card et al., 1999). Tapping into that channel would primarily entail appropriately exploiting visual strategies within the user interface.

The foregoing discussion points us to the field of *visual data mining*. There exist various definitions of visual data mining in the literature. "Visual data mining is the use of visualization techniques to allow data miners and analysts to evaluate, monitor, and guide the inputs, products and process of data mining" (Ganesh et al., 1996). Ankerst, M. (2000) defines visual data mining as "a step in the KD process that utilizes visualization as a communication channel between the computer and the user to produce novel and interpretable patterns." Kopanakis and Theodoulidis (2001) say that visual data mining "involves the invention of visual representations during all three data-mining life cycle stages, as partitioned to the data preparation, model derivation and validation stage." According to Simoff, S. (2001): "Visual data mining (Michalski et al., 1999) is an approach to explorative data analysis and knowledge discovery that is built on the extensive use of visual computing (Gross, M., 1994; Nielson et al., 1997). The basic assumption is that large and normally incomprehensible amounts of data can be reduced to a form that can be understood and interpreted by a human through the use of visualization techniques based on a particular metaphor or a combination of several metaphors (preferably, but not necessarily preserving the consistency of their combination)."

The field of visual data mining primarily revolves around the exploitation of the human visual system in mining knowledge. In essence, this can be realized by placing the user at a strategic place in the system framework while at the same time exploiting effective visual strategies/techniques. Visual data mining may, therefore, be defined as the exploitation of appropriate visual strategies/techniques in order to allow, enable, or empower the data mining user (such as data miners and analysts); to process data (and knowledge); and also to drive, guide or direct the entire process of data mining.

Besides the evident high-level benefits, namely: the exploitation of the human visual channel and allowing of the human user to guide the discovery process, visual data mining also offers various other specific benefits:

- The usage of effective visual strategies renders data mining systems user friendly, thereby opening up the system to a larger set of users rather than just the domain experts (Kopanakis and Theodoulidis, 2001).

- It is possible to make the data mining system include support for data-driven hypotheses generation and data mining (Kopanakis and Theodoulidis, 2001).

- The user can introduce suggestions and preferences in the earlier phases of data mining that may help reduce computation complexity. The user settings may also lead to increased quality in the data mining result, e.g., the result may contain much less amount of uninteresting data. In fact, the suggestions and preferences may turn out to be the basis for the development of better data mining processes and even algorithms (Ganesh et al., 1996; Kopanakis and Theodoulidis, 2001; André et al., 2007).

- Since the users are actively involved in the discovery process, they are much likely to trust results from the data mining process (Ankerst, M., 2000).

3.2.3   VISUAL DATA MINING APPROACH

Ankerst, M. (2000) highlights three approaches to visual data mining. Each approach is based on the mining stage at which the user is presented with a visualization. The approaches are visualization of the data mining result, visualization of an intermediate data mining result, and visualization of the data. In the "visualization of the data mining result" approach, the visualization resources are used primarily to present already processed/mined patterns. The data mining algorithm will have run, finished and returned the mining results/patterns. As for the "visualization of an intermediate data mining result" approach, the data mining algorithm starts the analysis of the target dataset but does not produce the final mining results/patterns. The user uses visualization resources to find interesting patterns from the intermediate mining results. In the "visualization of the data approach," the target dataset is visualized without the prior running of a sophisticated data mining algorithm on the data. The user primarily relies on visualization resources to explore the target dataset and find patterns that are of interest.

Another alternative approach that can be used to carry out visual data mining is based on the phases in the data mining process. The data mining process itself may be viewed as comprising three main phases: the data preparation phase, the model derivation phase, and the validation phase (Kopanakis and Theodoulidis, 2001). A visual data mining system should seek to incorporate the user into each of the three general phases. The system also should enable the user to take advantage of visual techniques in carrying out each and every activity related to the principal phases.

In the data preparation phase, there is the provision for visual preparation and manipulation of data. The data preprocessing activities should be carried out in accordance with the requirements posed by the phase and/or by the other data mining phases. Visual data mining also intends to support the derivation of the data mining model. The derivation involves activities such as the visual specification of the sample data set, visual specification of the model and its parameters, and visual support for the storage of results. In a more general sense, model derivation also involves other aspects such as evaluation, monitoring and guidance. Evaluation includes the validation of the sample data set and the developed models or algorithms. Monitoring includes, among other activities, keeping track of the progress of the data mining algorithms. Guidance entails activities such as the introduction of user-defined preferences or settings. Data mining algorithms are often able to handle large amounts of data. However, the size of the display is fixed and limited. Be that as it may, the results of data mining algorithms are often in a form that is difficult to understand by humans who are accustomed to perceiving information by their visual senses. The foregoing are major challenges in the validation phase of data mining. Through the appropriate use of effective visualizations, all relevant or at least much of the relevant data can be represented in an understandable manner. Consequently, visual data mining is instrumental in the validation phase in that it makes the provision for the user to acquire knowledge.

3.2.4   RELEVANT SYSTEMS

In the sequel, a discussion of some systems that are relevant to the field of visual data mining is given. The systems offer a reasonably great and diverse number of data mining and visualization functionalities.

Clementine[1] was developed by Integral Solutions Ltd (ISL), which was later purchased by SPSS. The product supports quite a number of mining techniques including the following: clustering, association rules, sequential patterns, factor analysis, and neural networks. Its visual interface reveals much about a data mining task by illustrating the flow of control and data. Therefore, the user is better positioned to understand and follow the mining process. Users construct a map of their data mining project/model called a "stream" by selecting icons, called "nodes" that represent steps in the data mining process. However, users would need to learn and think in terms of "streams" and "nodes." Moreover, the product does not fair very well in terms of scalability, i.e., Clementine does not scale up very well when dealing with massive amounts of data. It should be pointed out that

---

[1]http://www.spss.com/clementine

Clementine does allow users to adjust/refine their "streams" and rerun the system on the refined model. Figure 3.20 shows the visual interface.

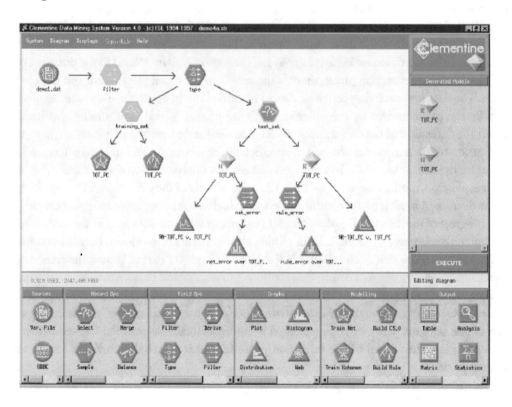

Figure 3.20: The visual interface of Clementine.

Enterprise Miner[2] is a product by the SAS Institute. The product provides diverse data mining algorithms such as: decision trees, neural networks, regression, radial basis functions, and clustering. The product offers extensive parameter options for the algorithms. Enterprise Miner has a reasonably interesting visual interface. However, the product is hard to use especially when compared with other products such as Clementine. Enterprise Miner has powerful support for data transformation. Its visualization tools are useful for multidimensional analysis. The effort does not report any studies explicitly designed for testing the usability of the product.

NicheWorks is a tool that was originally designed for exploring large graphs (Wills, G., 1997, 1999). Among other applications, the tool has been used to develop visualizations for detecting international calling frauds (Cox et al., 1997). The detection is basically realized by using a visualization of the calling activities that allows the system user to quickly notice unusual calling patterns.

[2]http://www.sas.com

The calling communities are represented using a directed graph, in which the nodes represent the subscribers whereas the links represent the calls. In particular, countries are mapped to unfilled circles, subscribers are represented by filled circles, the size and color of a filled circle reflect the total number of calls made by the subscriber. The width and color of a link represent the overall level of communication between the two ends. The tool also enables the user to drill-down on suspected patterns. It should be pointed out that, in the real sense of the word, NicheWorks is not a data mining system; it may be regarded as a visualization or exploratory tool. Therefore, the tool cannot fully accommodate the entire mining process. Nonetheless, the tool is a classic example of the role of visual data mining in visualizing raw data.

DBMiner[3] is an OLAP data mining system developed by the Data Mining Research Group from the Intelligent Database Systems Research Laboratory at Simon Fraser University (Han et al., 1996). The system is owned by DBMiner Technology Inc[4]. It supports association rules, meta-patterns, classification, and clustering. DBMiner provides a browser to visualize the OLAP process. Association rules are visualized using bar charts and a three-dimensional ball graph view. With regard to visualizing decision trees, the product offers a three-dimensional graph view and an optional grid view. Clustering results are visualized using a two-dimensional graph view or a grid view. The user interface is fairly simple and standard. However, it should be pointed out that users who are not acquainted with data mining are likely to find the data mining environment somewhat intimidating. It should be acknowledged that DBMiner does interface with MS-OLAP Server and also uses MS-Excel as a browser for visualizing the OLAP process. Nonetheless, DBMiner provides no explicit support for data/results export and import. Moreover, the effort does not report any evaluation on the system.

KnowledgeSTUDIO is a product by ANGOSS Software Corporation[5]. The product supports decision trees, clustering, and neural networks. Decision trees can be constructed automatically or interactively. The product relies heavily on standard business applications (e.g., MS Office) for visualization functionalities. Due to its interactive and exploratory environment, data mining models can be produced with relative ease. Consequently, KnowledgeSTUDIO has a short learning curve. The product presently does not offer an explicit recourse for exporting data mining results (or for exchanging data mining models in general). However, it is should observed that its support for Predictive Model Markup Language (PMML) could facilitate export of results. There is no record of any usability studies carried out on the product. The visual interface can be seen in Figure 3.21.

Another effort relevant to the field of visual data mining is *VisMine* (Hao et al., 1999a,b) that is based on the premise that new techniques for mining knowledge from large data warehouses often exhibit the following problems: display problems (cluttered display and disjoint displays), limited access, and lack of expandability. The main features of VisMine are: hiding non-primary structures and relationships, unless the user focuses on them; supporting the simultaneous presentation of multiple visual presentations ('slice and dice'); and providing architectural plug-in support to enable

[3]http://db.cs.sfu.ca
[4]http://www.dbminer.com
[5]http://www.angoss.com

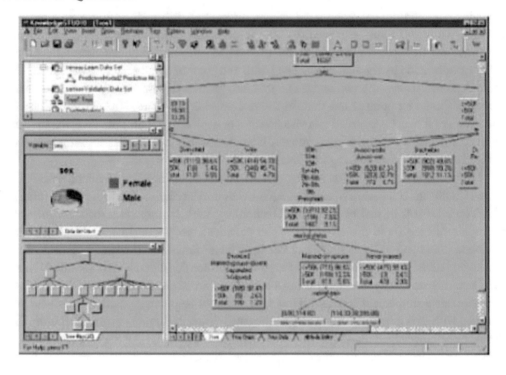

Figure 3.21: The visual interface of KnowledgeSTUDIO.

the exploitation of other visualization toolkits. The infrastructure is more of a visual exploration environment than a core data mining system.

TempleMVV (Mihalisin and Timlin, 1995) may be traced back to MVV (Mihalisin et al., 1991). The latter uses bar charts (histogram within histogram within histogram) and slide bars (with horizontal scales) to locate clusters in multidimensional space that allows the display of multiple views of a given dataset. TempleMVV is a tool that has been proposed for fast visual data mining. It provides hierarchical visualizations for any mix of categorical and continuous attributes. Its visualization paradigm is based on nested attributes, with four attributes being represented at the same time.

VidaMine is a visual data mining system that aims at providing the user with a consistent, uniform, flexible and intuitive visual interaction environment in order to allow or enable the user not only to process data but also to steer, guide or direct the entire process of mining knowledge (Kimani et al., 2008). Its visual interface offers visual interaction environments across different mining techniques and tasks. At present, the system offers visual environments for mining meta-queries, performing clustering, and mining association rules. Each visual environment comprises six visual parts/sections. Each visual part corresponds to some mining subtask such as the construction of target dataset, the selection of a data mining algorithm, the visualization of mining results, etc.

Three visual parts of the visual environment are used for specifying various exploration and mining parameters. The parts are: Specification Space, Target Space, and a part through which a user specifies/sets parameters for a particular data mining strategy. The other three visual parts are views for the visualization of data. The data could simply be the target data or the results of a mining task. The views are: Overview, Detail, and Dedicated View. Figure 3.22, which is for the Metaquery Environment, shows the overall outlook of the visual interface. From an architectural point of view, the system is open and has a modular structure with well defined change/extension points.

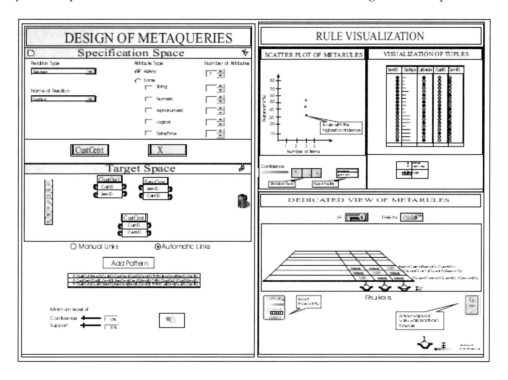

Figure 3.22: The overall outlook of VidaMine.

3.2.5   CHALLENGES AND ISSUES

The field of visual data mining faces many challenges and exhibits various issues that need to be addressed. These are discussed in the sequel.

Visual support often necessitates the use of graphical elements. The user is expected to interact with these graphics in real time. Interaction with graphics in real time often places demands on the computer memory, thereby negatively affecting the performance of the system. Consequently, the visual environment may not immediately reflect changes occurring in the underlying dataset in real time. It is no trivial task to determine a good balance between interactivity and performance.

Data mining methods normally handle complex data. Since visual data mining systems integrate data mining techniques and visualization techniques, visualization techniques have to seek effective visual mappings in order to represent the complex relationships in data.

Most of the existing visual data mining systems have not been subjected to thorough usability tests. In order to determine the usefulness of visual data mining systems, the importance of usability studies cannot be overemphasized. On the same note, it is worth acknowledging that the lack of precise theory or a universal/standard framework for developing visual data mining systems may not only be partly responsible for the current situation whereby each visual data mining system seems to be an ad-hoc development but may also, to some extent at least, complicate the usability issue as far as the visual data mining field is concerned.

It is a challenging activity to find the methods, techniques, and corresponding tools that are suitable for a specific visual mining task or a particular type of data. One way forward would be to evaluate the disparate frameworks to determine their effectiveness and to verify their applicability in different application domains (Simoff, S., 2001).

CHAPTER 4

More Advanced Applications

Databases and related applications no longer only deal with alphanumeric records. They contain several kinds of heterogeneous data distributed in multiple sources. The same is true for the devices used to access them that are not just desktop computers but are becoming more and more mobile and ubiquitous.

4.1   WEB DATA

As in so many areas, the web is changing the nature of data access. For some application areas it is a relatively small change: SQL databases are used to drive web interfaces instead of client-server applications and may be hosted on the cloud. There are changes in practices because web user interfaces are different from desktop ones, but this is not fundamentally about the data.

However, there are also more fundamental changes: data that were once in government or corporate databases are made publically available, user-generated content proliferates, mashups integrate, and the semantic web seeks to link all the world's data. This is, perhaps, not surprising as the world-wide web was developed precisely as a means of distributing data.

4.1.1   THE CHANGING FACE OF THE WEB

The web is now a place to meet friends, browse news, book holidays, or find read information. However, the world-wide web was originally designed for sharing the data of CERN (Berners-Lee, T., 1999), and it has become a critical part of many organizations information systems.

The web has evolved continuously since the early 1990s, but it can be seen in terms of three phases, each with very different kinds of data (described in more detail in the next Section 4.1.2):

First Generation Web – The first generation web (sometimes called web1.0) is characterized by familiar HTML pages and links. This first generation web gave rise to early home-made web pages, but it became quickly dominated by traditional 'publishing' models, with the majority of the volume of viewed content being produced by a small number of large companies. The data of this first generation web was mostly focused at human consumption: images, text, occasionally sound, and movies, although often scientific and technical data are also available as downloadable files it tends to sit at the 'edge' of the web, not an interlinked part of it. More structured data were there, in the form of databases for eCommerce and other back-end data, but this was largely invisible behind web user interfaces.

Second Generation Web (web2.0) – The term web2.0 was popularized in 2005 by Tim O'Reilly's article "What Is Web 2.0" (O'Reilly, T., 2005) and the founding of the web2.0 conference. The term was not inventing a new web, but putting a name to a number of emerging trends. Often web2.0 is identified with a number of technologies, principally AJAX (Holdener, A., 2008) and modifiable DOM (Goodman, D., 2006), which allowed far more expressive user interfaces on the web. However, more disruptive was the change in the nature of information production on the web. While the kinds of data were similar to the first generation web (text, images, and movies), sites such as YouTube and Wikipedia changed the locus of control from a few central 'publishers' to the mass of web users. This was in fact part of the original concept for the web and indeed, the reason for the often-ignored 'PUT' method in HTTP, but it somehow lost along the way. In other ways too, the web2.0 emphasizes a more dynamic and end-user focus from the 'perpetual beta' of web software production, to Google AdSense, which allowed advertising on the 'long tail' of tiny web sites with small numbers of very specialised readers. From a data point of view, the most obvious new thing in web2.0 is the rise of tagging (e.g., in tags on photos in Flickr[1]) and the emerging folksonomies (see the next Section 4.1.2), as compared to the hand-edited taxonomies of Yahoo! and other first generation portals. However, one of O'Reilly's list of characterizing features of web2.0 is "Harnessing Collective Intelligence," which included both 'front end' information such as Wikipedia, but also 'back end' data processing such as Amazon's book recommendations.

Next Generation: the semantic web and web3.0 – It is easier to recount the past than predict the future; however, there is a growing movement towards a new generation of the web that exploits data semantics, that is machine readable data that can be 'mashed up' to make applications unthought-of of by the publishers of the data. Semantic web (Berners-Lee et al., 2001) seeks to make more of the meaning of the web available for machine processing. While this has so far been largely aspirational and the subject of academic papers rather than real applications, it has started to become mainstream especially since several governments including the UK and USA have made public data available in RDF – the central technology of the semantic web. Some are looking towards the future convergence of the semantic web with the social power of web2.0 and calling this next wave web3.0 although the term has almost as many different interpretations as web2.0.

4.1.2   UNDERSTANDING WEB DATA

What is on the Web
Web data come from a variety of sources:

Conventional Data – Standard corporate data that are being accessed via a web interface. For example, LOTUS Notes has been available via a web interface for more than 10 years, and, virtually, all major business applications, such as SAP, either have web interfaces or are accessed solely through intranet or extranets on the web.

Published Web-of Data – Many organizations are publishing data that previously would have been either deliberately secret or made available through pre-digested publishing such as reports. For example, the City of London has made crime data available online, allowing third parties to create mash-ups and visualizations.

---

[1]http://www.flickr.com/

Informal User-Generated Content – From Flickr and YouTube[2] to blogs and tweets, many of the web's largest businesses derive their value from user's own media and data. This is one of the hallmarks of web 2.0 and harnessing this data effectively can make the difference between success and failure of these businesses.

Structured End-User Data – While the majority of end-user content is unstructured rich-media or text, there are also a variety of applications where users enter more structured information. Often this is in pre-structured forms such as a Facebook[3] profile. This may be used only internally within a single web site or web application, or it may be made available to third-party applications via separate data feeds such as the social networking site hi5[4], which uses FOAF (friend-of-a-friend) ontology in its API (see Figure 4.1) or as embedded micro-formats.

```
– <rdf:RDF>
  – <foaf:Person rdf:nodeID="me">
      <foaf:nick>Dave</foaf:nick>
      <foaf:givenName>Dave</foaf:givenName>
      <foaf:surName>Brondsema</foaf:surName>
      <foaf:mboxSha1Sum>76961c2c7e0e47858e041aa4968c7257f451c45d</foaf:mboxSha1Sum>
      <foaf:birthday>2-5</foaf:birthday>
      <foaf:img rdf:resource="http://images.hi5.com/images/nophoto_boy_100.gif"/>
      <foaf:weblog rdf:resource="http://www.hi5.com/profile/displayJournal.do?userid=39290024"/>
      <foaf:gender>male</foaf:gender>
      <foaf:homePage rdf:resource="http://www.hi5.com/friend/profile/displayProfile.do?userid=39290024"/>
    – <foaf:knows>
      – <foaf:Person>
          <foaf:nick>Lucero</foaf:nick>
          <rdfs:seeAlso rdf:resource="http://api.hi5.com/rest/profile/foaf/39301767"/>
        </foaf:Person>
      </foaf:knows>
    </foaf:Person>
  </rdf:RDF>
```

Figure 4.1: hi5 REST API (Fielding, R., 2000) using FOAF (Brickley and Miller, 2000).

Meta-Data – Large amounts of data are gathered about the web itself, from basic web logs to search engine click-through data and eCommerce transaction records. This is not just for diagnostic or audit purposes, but it is often the heart of web-based business value, for example, Amazon's use of purchasing and viewing information to suggest books.

Types of Web Data
Web data are also of various kinds:

[2]http://www.youtube.com/
[3]http://www.facebook.com/
[4]http://hi5.com/

tabular – Much of the conventional data published on the web or used to drive web-based interfaces are in traditional SQL databases. Furthermore, even new forms of web data are often tabular: for example, Facebook offers a data API to developers which is basically tables, HTML5 and Google Gears allow web applications to store local information in SQL, and Freebase[5] allows end-user content in the form of tables.

text – Of course, when we think of the web, the primary image is HTML and pages of text (and pictures). In addition, blogs and microblogs such as Twitter or Facebook status updates are primarily or solely text-based.

rich media – Many web 2.0 sites, such as Flickr and YouTube, contain user generated media as well as pictures and various media.

links – The essence of the web is its links. Importantly these add structure to the web, which can be used to simply surf or as a source of data to be mined – the source of Google's success.

tags – Whereas older portals used hierarchical structures, end-user sites such as del.icio.us and Flickr are based on tagging. In addition to being less formal, social sites allow serendipitous connections between similarly tagged material and the emergence of community vocabularies known as "folksonomies."

XML, RDF and semantic-web data – Various forms of structured data can often be found either in standalone documents or embedded in HTML. These formats are designed to be machine readable to encode information or meta-data, but they use textual formats so that they are in principle viewable or editable. These are described later in Section 4.1.4.

micro-formats – Micro-formats offer a form of 'nearly for free' semantics using lightweight additional mark-up in a human readable web page. For example, Figure 4.2 shows a fragment of the source of Alan's LinkedIn profile page. Note the <span> tag with class "given-name" so that a web crawler or browser with a suitable plug-in can work out what "Alan" means.

```
<div class="masthead vcard contact">
  <div id="nameplate">
    <h1 id="name">
      <span class="fn n">
          <span class="given-name">Alan</span>
          <span class="family-name">Dix</span>
      </span>
    </h1>
  </div>
```

Figure 4.2: Linkedin using vCard microformat.

[5]http://www.freebase.com

4.1.3   EXAMPLES OF END-USER WEB DATA INTERFACES

We all interact with web data whenever we use Amazon or make an online booking, and most blogs are implemented over a backend SQL database. However, sometimes the data are more 'up front,' enabling one to see that there is a database behind the scenes.

One example of this is Swivel (see Figure 4.3), which allows end-users to enter tabular data and then visualize them using a variety of charts. The key 'web' feature of Swivel is the focus on allowing users to share numeric and tabular data on the web just as pictures are shared in Flickr.

Figure 4.3: Swivel – tabular data (`www.swivel.com`).

A similar application is Freebase (Figure 4.4). It also allows users to enter and share data, but unlike tabular data used in Swivel and Google docs, it is based on an ontology. That is, in Swivel and Google docs, the meaning of the data in the tables is only available in human-readable form of column headings. In contrast, in Freebase users can add data to standard base classes such as People or Places, or they can create their own classes and relationships. This means that the data in Freebase are linked to each other – if one user adds data on famous Latvian authors including their place of birth, then the birth town can be linked to data that another user has entered about Latvian towns.

Structured data can also occur in web pages that are primarily intended to be human readable. We have already mentioned micro-formats and will return to them later. However, anything that has some form of structure can also be available as a data source. A well-known example is Wikipedia, which is primarily designed for people to read. However, for certain sorts of pages, including those describing places, airports and software applications, there is an 'info box' on the right-hand side that has structured data. For example, Figure 4.5 shows the web page for the island of Tiree and in the info box are its population, land area, and the local government authority.

Figure 4.4: Freebase - ontology-based data (`www.freebase.com`).

Because this information is structured, it is available for machine processing. The project DBpedia has done precisely this, creating an RDF repository from the Wikipedia info boxes. This can then be mixed with other online data or queried on its own using the RDF query language SPARQL (see Figure 4.6).

Not all data are textual or numerical – maps and geographic information have become increasingly important on the web. Whereas GIS (geographic information systems) used to be a very specialised area of database systems, the combination of mapping mash-ups such as Google maps and GPS availability on mobile phones and digital cameras have led to map-focused interactions becoming commonplace. Some of this information comes from traditional mapping and GIS data sources; however, others come from more 'web-like' sources: Google finds addresses in web pages and OpenStreeMap uses a Wikipedia-like model, inviting anyone to add features to its maps (see Figure 4.7), which are then available to all through a Creative Commons licence.

4.1.4   WEB TECHNOLOGY AND THE WEB OF DATA

The web has spawned many technologies, but most significant for data management are XML, RDF, and (currently) to a lesser extent OWL.

Both XML and RDF were technologies originally designed for one purpose and then appropriated for another. XML was a text markup notation based on a restricted variant of SGML, which was originally designed for the publishing industry. Whereas SGML documents required a data description (a DTD) to be parsed, XML was designed to be syntactically *self-describing*, thus being more robust in the open web environment. One example of this is the hierarchical structure of tags.

Figure 4.5: Wikipedia page including info box on right.

```
PREFIX dbprop: <http://dbpedia.org/property/>
PREFIX db: <http://dbpedia.org/resource/>
SELECT ?who ?work ?genre
WHERE {
        db:Tokyo_Mew_Mew dbprop:illustrator ?who .
        ?work    dbpprop:author ?who .
        OPTIONAL { ?work dbpprop:genre ?genre } .
      }
```

Figure 4.6: SPARQL query of DBpedia RDF (from `wikipedia.org/wiki/dbpedia`).

Early HTML had been derived from SGML and so, for example, close tags were not required where they could be inferred from the structure, for example, in "<ul><li>one<li>two</ul>," a parser knows that the first <li> tag encloses "one" as <li> elements cannot be nested, effectively yielding "<ul><li>one</li><li>two</li></ul>," not "<ul><li>one<li>two</li></li></ul>." This is fine for a well-known structure such as HTML, but it means that new tags cannot easily be added. In contrast, XML enforces strict nesting, so a parser does not need to know the kind of data to be able to parse the hierarchical structure. A DTD can be associated with an XML document; however, this can be used optionally for validation and is not essential for parsing.

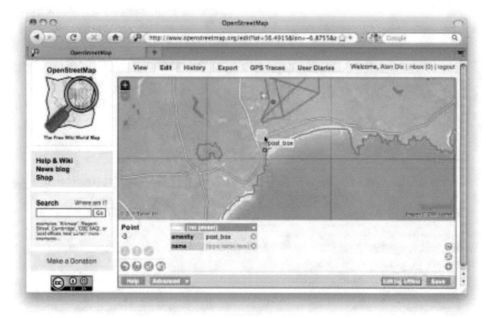

Figure 4.7: OpenStreetMap – end user adding a feature.

This self-describing nature has meant that XML has been adopted widely on the web not just as a text mark-up notation but as, effectively, a data serialization. For example, Figure 4.8 shows XML being used to package together information about this book. XML has several problems when used in this way. Some are trivial yet serious, such as the lack of a standard way to include a tab character in XML data. Others are more subtle, such as the confusion between slot/variable name and type.

```
<book>
    <name>User-Centered Data Management</name>
    <author>Tiziana Catarci</author>
    <author>Stephen Kimani</author>
    <author>Giuseppe Santucci</author>
    <author>Alan Dix</author>
</book>
```

Figure 4.8: Describing this book in XML.

There has been significant work on the use of XML in databases; however, the greatest use has been either as a data transfer format between web services, invisible to the user, or as an intermediate format in web systems with a multi-tier (also known as n-tier) architecture. In these multi-tier architectures, the lower-level modules respond to a user request by producing an XML document with the key data required as a response. A higher level subsequently transforms this into a web page using XSLT, a notation that allows generic descriptions of transformations of XML to other formats, notably HTML. This multi-layer approach is similar to the presentation-functionality separation found in traditional pre-web user interface architectures such as Seeheim (Pfaff and ten Hagen, 1985) and MVC (Krasner and Pope, 1988).

RDF (Resource Description Framework) was originally developed as a way to add semantics to web pages such as the page author (Powers, S., 2003; W3C, 2010). This is possible to do inside a web page using the <meta> and <link> tags in the page header, but this means that you have to have the whole web page to hand and, furthermore, that the information has been entered fully and correctly by the page author. RDF allows information to be described separate from the page itself, maybe added by a third party. However, RDF has been adopted more widely as a knowledge representation framework by assigning URIs to non-web resources such as people, books and countries. (Note, URIs, not necessarily URLs, uniquely *identify* the resources but may not point to an actual *location* on the web.)

Figure 4.9 shows a short RDF description of this book. The data is represented a as series of triples: <subject, predicate, object>, where each triple tells you some property of the subject. For example, the triple with predicate 'dc:title' has subject (what it is about) 'mc:ucdm' and object "User-Centered Data Management." While this is a minimalist representation compared to tables in a relational database or the hierarchical structure of XML, in fact, anything that can be represented in either tables or XML can also be described (albeit verbosely) in triples.

```
@prefix mcb:   <http://www.morganclaypool.com/books/> .
@prefix dc:    <http://purl.org/dc/elements/1.1/> .
mcb:ucdm   dc:title    "User-Centered Data Management" .
mcb:ucdm   dc:author   "Giuseppe Santucci" .
mcb:ucdm   dc:author   "Stephen Kimani" .
mcb:ucdm   dc:author   "Alan Dix" .
mcb:ucdm   dc:author   "Tiziana Catarci" .
```

Figure 4.9: Describing this book in RDF (N3 notation).

While XML requires that all the data are lumped together, RDF allows knowledge to be represented in fragments and pieced together as needed. For example, Figure 4.10 has some additional information about the book, and this could be located in a completely different repository. This is particularly valuable in the open environment of the web where different sources may bring different data.

Note that Figure 4.10 also shows the use of 'dc:title' (shorthand for 'http://purl.org/dc/elements/1.1/#title') from the Dublin Core ontology. By using a commonly known ontology, this makes it possible for computer tools to understand the meaning of the properties. Note also that some of the triples defined simple properties of an entity, such as the name of the book, while others denote a relationship between two entities, for example, that the book belongs to a particular series.

```
@prefix dc:   <http://purl.org/dc/elements/1.1/> .
<http://www.morganclaypool.com/books/#ucdm>
      <#inseries>
            <http://www.morganclaypool.com/series/#sldm> .
<http://www.morganclaypool.com/series/#sldm>
      dc:title  "Synthesis Lectures in Data Management" .
<http://www.morganclaypool.com/books/#ucdm>
      <#place>
            <http://www.geonames.org/countries/US/> .
```

Figure 4.10: Additional triples about this book.

The latter means that in general RDF describes a graph or network not simply flat or tree-structured data.

Finally, and perhaps most important, the fragment in Figure 4.10 includes an external URI to a resource in the Geonames data set. By using a URI rather than a string "USA" means that different RDF datasets can be easily linked together. The collection of web-accessible interlinked RDF data sets is called "linked data" (Bizer et al., 2009; Harel, D., 1988) or simply the "web of data" (WoD), and it is rapidly growing. Figure 4.11 shows a snapshot of the data sets in 2008, including DBpedia, the RDF version of Wikipedia, and Geonames, which gathers a wide rage of geographical data. Now the picture is beginning to get too complex to show in a simple graphic.

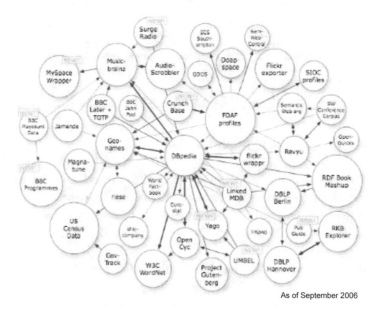

As of September 2006

Figure 4.11: The web of linked data (based on Heath, T., 2008).

For the application developer, this offers a wealth of information that can be brought together, and then for the end-user, the resulting data mash-ups offer different ways of looking at the same data.

4.1.5   INTERACTING WITH THE WEB OF DATA

While the web of data (WoD) is growing rapidly, it is still the exception on the web, with most pages containing primarily human readable information. However, we can also see applications that are in some way related to or linked into the growing WoD.

These WoD applications can be categorised in two ways:

- *User Sees the WoD* – Some applications actively present a view to the user that looks like linked semantic resources, while other applications hide the underlying data representation with some form of bespoke view, for example, taking RDF data on crime statistics and presenting it as icons on a map. This is similar to traditional relational databases where administrators see the database directly in terms of tables, schema, and records, but most end-users only see the database indirectly through application user interfaces, maybe a shopping catalogue or bank statement.

- *Implemented Using WoD* – Some are based on underlying semantic web standards, while others use traditional technology or non-standard ontologies

This leads to four main classes of WoD applications (see Figure 4.12), which we will deal with in turn.

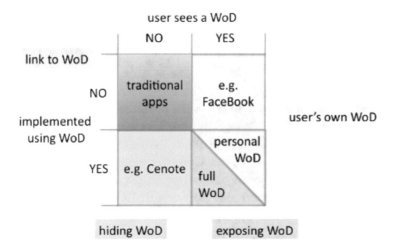

Figure 4.12: Accessing the web of data.

Exposing the Web of Data

The most obvious WoD interfaces are semantic web visualizations that expose linked data directly to the user. The iconic example of this is Tabulator, Berners-Lee's group's own RDF browser (Berners-Lee et al., 2006). Tabulator allows users to browse RDF using a hierarchical interface where properties of a URI can be viewed on a page, the links from those properties either drilled into outliner-style, or opened on a page of their own. The example in Figure 4.13, shows properties of a portion of RDF describing the Tabulator project itself.

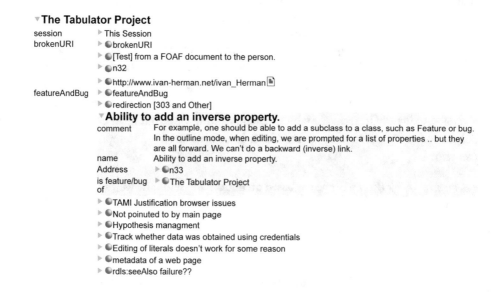

Figure 4.13: Tabulator – outliner style + query list views + editing. `http://dig.csail.mit.edu/2005/ajar/release/tabulator/0.8/tab.html`

The left-hand column in Figure 4.13 shows the predicates describing the Tabulator project; some of these have a single object (e.g., session) and some have several (e.g., BrokenURI). Some of the properties refer to internal nodes in the RDF graph, but some (e.g., `http://www.ivan-hermen.net/Ivan_Herman`) link to external resources. One of the properties "Ability to add an inverse property" has been expanded inline showing its own predicates, including one triple with predicate 'comment' where the object is literal text rather than another RDF node.

Note that while RDF describes a graph, the Tabulator visualization is a tree that roots the graph at a particular node; in particular, this means the same node may appear several times in the displayed tree. Some visualizations try to show the graph more directly using a 2D visualization; however, the size of RDF graphs means that attempts to visualize the whole graph rapidly becomes cumbersome unless there is some form of information reduction such as clustering. Most commonly, visualizations are focused on a single node and its close neighbours.

Text based visualizations also often take this node focus approach. For example, the FOAF Explorer visualizes friend-of-a-friend (FOAF) data (Fielding, R., 2000), which is a way of describing people and their personal relationships using RDF. Figure 4.14 shows FOAF data for Tim Berners-Lee. Links to other people are live linking through to their own FOAF visualization, just like navigating web pages. Note how different properties are rendered differently; for example, all the people are in the block entitled 'Knows,' highlighted with a blue background as navigating these is central to the FOAF Explorer's use, while predicates such as 'title' are displayed as plain lists, and the image is positioned to the right and shown as an image not a URL.

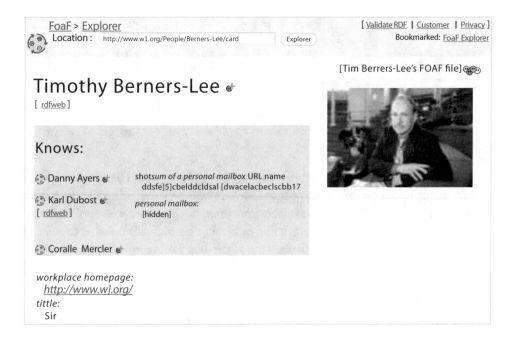

Figure 4.14: FOAF Explorer – drill-down / link style, part bespoke. `http://xml.mfd-consult.dk/foaf/explorer/`

Tabulator is a generic interface that can handle any RDF data whatsoever and thus has 'vanilla' style, while FOAF Explorer is focused on a particular kind of data and particular style of use (exploring people), and so it has a more bespoke visualization. Tabulator has the ability to plug-in templates for particular kinds of data, so that, for example, FOAF data could be displayed more like FOAF explorer does, or countries could be displayed with their maps. Even to create the vanilla listing, Tabulator needs to select a particular property of a node to use as its display name; otherwise, the display in Figure 4.13 would consist almost purely of fairly obscure URIs. However, note there is a difference between tailoring displays to the *kind of data* and tailoring them to the intended purpose.

Both Tabulator and FOAF Explorer are focused on exploring from one node and moving out. Others are more focused on filtering the mass of data to find suitable collections of nodes. One example is mSpace, which is a framework for creating *faceted* browsers for different kinds of data. For example, Figure 4.15 shows three properties: its genre, decade and director, being used to select a set of movies that have particular set of values: Film-Noir, 1950s, Allen, Lewis.

Figure 4.15: mSpace – facets for selecting a movie. http://www.iam.ecs.soton.ac.uk/projects/292.html

Figure 4.16 shows mSpace applied to a data set describing music. The user has gotten as far as a particular set of composers and then selected Mozart who is viewed using a custom style.

When data have explicit machine-readable semantics, it is possible for an application to know that a particular property represents a date, color, or place. This makes it possible to offer ways to visualize or browse data tuned to the particular type of the data; for example, Tabulator offers a map view, and mSpace has a method of viewing rich timelines (André et al., 2007).

Hiding the Web of Data

As a developer or low-level user of web data, it is important to be able to see a fairly raw view of the underlying data; that is a view that explicitly represents the individual URLs, properties, and relationships. Also, if one wants to be able to explore data in unexpected ways, one may need much of its structure to be readily available. However, for most purposes, end users don't care about the precise form of the underlying data; they just want to do things. Of course, the things they want to do often include accessing the information represented by the underlying data, but they don't care whether their friend's list is stored in RDF, XML, or a plain text file.

This is just the same in relational database systems; end-users are not offered a bare SQL command-line, but usually they have some sort of graphical interface on top of the data. The same is true of web data. Figure 4.17 shows Ceenote, mash-up of data concerning books from a variety of sources linked together to create a single interface. The user is unaware of the web data beneath the surface; this is just a way of viewing books, but 'under the bonnet' the power of web technology is being applied to create the linkages. To some extent, the ISBN already acts as a way of linking the relevant data sources together, but, in fact, the team had to do extra work to enable some of the data

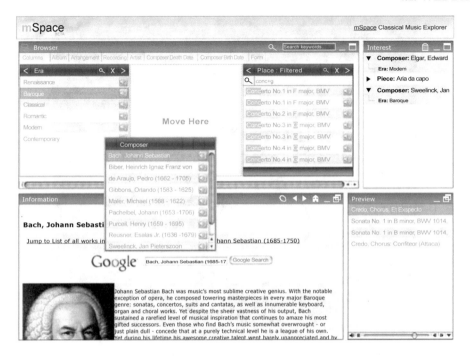

Figure 4.16: mSpace – faceted browsing of a music dataset. `http://mspace.fm/`

to be linked. For example, older books may not have an ISBN, and also the same book, for example, 'Tom Sawyer,' will have different ISBNs if printed by different publishers; while these are different variants or editions, they are still in some senses 'the same,' at least for some purposes – if you want to borrow 'Tom Sawyer' from the library, you normally don't care which publisher or print run.

User's Own Web of Data

Sometimes users are presented with data that are similar to web data and, indeed, may be presented on the web, but are in on some way isolated. One example of this is in Facebook. There is a clear web of relationships; people can be friends of other people, and they can be named in pictures, so it is possible to navigate from a person to pictures naming that person, to the people who posted the picture, to their friends.

Furthermore, Facebook offers developers an API that allows them to create their own classes of data (tables) and relationships (see Figure 4.18). For example, a developer might create a task management application with tasks and to-dos as tables with a 'sub-task' relationship between tasks and a 'responsible for' relationship between to-dos and people.

For a variety of reasons, partly their users' privacy, partly commercial protection, Facebook only allows linking into Facebook standard classes and does not allow rich links among application data

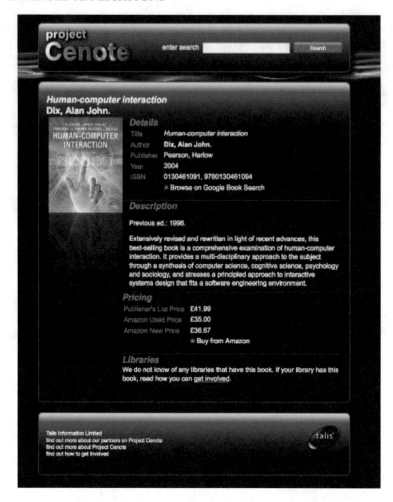

Figure 4.17:   Ceenote – rich interfaces on top of linked data (http://cenote.talis.com/).

and between application data and the web. There are some Facebook applications that circumvent this, for example, publishing friends data as FOAF, but strictly, they are breaking Facebook's terms and conditions.

There are signs that this is changing, and Facebook is becoming more open; however, this example of Facebook data underlines some of the social and commercial issues surrounding linked web data. From the point of view of the users, they may want control over their personal information, being able to move it between applications. However, commercial interests may work against this as companies seek to retain a hold on users' data.

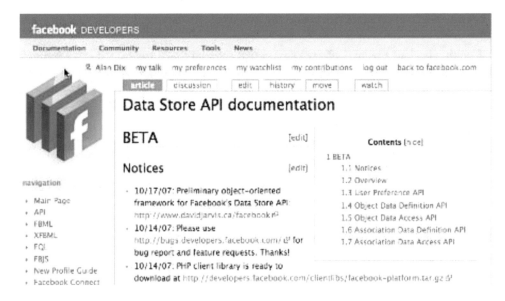

Figure 4.18: Facebook Data Store API (`http://wiki.developers.facebook.com/`).

The area of "semantic desktop" research also creates web-like data that is relatively disconnected from the wider web. The various projects in this area are attempting to use semantic web technology for desktop-based systems. They typically mine the user's files, email, address book, etc. and put the information into RDF triples. This can then be explored using ontology-based tools or used to augment desktop applications using plug-ins. For example, when viewing a file, one might be shown links to the person who created the file, and through that email form that person.

This web of personal data is often called a personal ontology. It will start with standard classes such as date, person, project, and event and may allow the user to add classes of their own, for example, sub-classing 'events' to include 'raves.' Most importantly, the ontology's classes are populated with the user's own data.

The personal ontology may also include links to external resources; for example, countries may link through a GeoNames URI to DBpedia entries for that country. However, the links are one way and other people would not normally be allowed to look inside each other's personal ontologies.

Clearly, there are times when it would be useful to be able to connect one's information, for example, in a commercial organisation or even at home to link information on friend's addresses. However, there are technical and user interface barriers. At the technical level, some of the classes that might be found in a personal ontology, such as 'Family' is egocentric; Tiziana's 'Family' is not the same as Alan's 'Family.' Mapping between ontologies is a difficult problem for knowledge engineers, let alone ordinary users. At an interaction level, one needs to be able specify what can and cannot be shared. For tabular data, it is relatively easy to allow access to a particular collection or for hierarchies to open up a folder; however, for a network, the bounds of what is acceptable for sharing are hard to define.

Looking back at Figure 4.12, we can see that the user's own web of data cuts across two of the quadrants. Applications like Facebook are clearly in the top right quadrant; they allow the user to see a form of web of relationships, but underneath, they are not using semantic web technology. However, whilst personal ontologies do use semantic web technology, they are not fully linked to web data. Although it is easy to focus on particular W3C standard technologies, such as RDF, as being core, in fact the most crucial thing about web data is that it is linked, that is, forms a web. The use of standardised technologies facilitates that linking, but it is the linking itself that matters.

Link to the Web of Data

Referring again to Figure 4.12, the top right quadrant, labelled 'link to WoD,' looks as if it is totally disconnected from the web of data. However, even plain HTML web pages can be linked to the semantic web. This is very important; there are some rich web services available that fully use semantic web technologies, but most web pages and applications do not!

In order to link this plain web content to the web of data, some level of semantics needs to be present; otherwise, no linking is possible. This can be quite limited mark-up added by the web developer or web server at the *point of creation*. Alternatively, it may even be added later at the *point of use* when the end-user accesses the content, for example, by some sort of automatic recognition in the end-user's web browser.

We have already seen an example of the former with the use of micro-formats. These basically take portions of text content and add mark-up to signal what kind of data they are, such as contact information or event. This was introduced earlier as a source of web data, but it can also be a way to interact with the web of data. If a piece of text is marked up as a country name, then a web browser with a suitable plug-in can link the country name to the Geonames URI for the country and hence to the whole web of linked data.

```
<p class="vcard">Hi, my name is <span class="fn">Jamie
Jones</span> and I dig microformats!</p>
```

Figure 4.19: Microformat example (from `http://www.microformats.org`).

Micro-formats usually tag textual information, so to be used, they need to be looked up in suitable directories (such as Geonames for the country name). Semantic web purists prefer linking id through URIs; however, this typically requires more work and a savvy content editor or some form of properly semantic-web enabled editor. However, web pages are always full of links anyway, and so these can be used as entry points into the web of data. One tool doing this is zLinks, a Wordpress plug-in that adds linked-data annotations to every link (Bergman and Giasson, 2008); the content creator merely needs to add ordinary links when creating a blog post. However, as most web pages do not have explicit semantic web links, the end-user still has to be fairly careful about what links are chosen in order to have useful annotations.

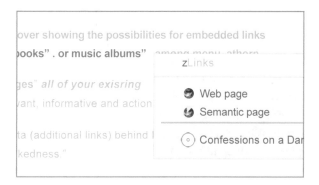

Figure 4.20: zLinks Wordpress plug-in (from `http://zitgist.com/products/zlink`).

Where there is no annotation at all, text-mining techniques can be used to find suitable points that can link the text to semantic resources. The earliest example of this is in the pre-web Hypertext system Microcosm (Hall et al., 1996). Most Hypertext systems, at that point (and HTML web pages today), relied on the author of the source page to add some sort of link to the target material. However, this means that the hypertext linking is limited to the author's knowledge of the potential material at the point of creation; if the author does not know everything that could be linked to, or if the material changes, then the authored material is incomplete or out of date. Microcosm instead used automatic *external linkage*: the page author did not worry about what was going to be linked to but instead, simply chose key words and terms for the document; then when any other document used those terms they became live links. For example, imagine a variant of Wikipedia, the authors never create links, but every mention of "Edgar Codd" in the text is automatically converted into a link to "`http://en.wikipedia.org/wiki/Edgar_F._Codd`." As well as hand authored material, this could be used by the server to create links to more structured material, for example, in a University system, course codes in meeting minutes could be linked to the relevant course documentation, or in a commercial setting, product codes linked to the product information or ordering system.

This same principle of external linkage can be found in a class of systems called *data detectors* that were originally developed in the late 1990s, including the Intel selection recognition agent (Pandit and Kalbag, 1997), Apple Data Detectors (Nardi et al., 1998), Georgia Tech's CyberDesk (Wood et al., 1997), and aQtive onCue (Dix et al., 2000). Data detectors work by examining some aspect of the user current context and then suggesting possible actions based on that. For example, most current email applications recognise URLs embedded in the email message and turn these into live links, and they are a form of primitive data detector. Data detectors also recognise other features such as dates, names or postal codes and use these to create links to desktop or web resources. For example, if a name is detected the user might be directed to a web service to lookup telephone numbers. A number of systems have developed in this area in more recent years including Microsoft Smart Tags, a clipboard converter Citrine (Stylos et al., 2004), and web based tools CREO (Faaborg and Lieberman, 2006), and Snip!t (Dix et al., 2006; Dix, A., 2008).

The early data detector systems depended almost entirely on syntactic matching. For example, Apple Data Detectors used a BNF-like syntax and many onCue recognizers were based on regular expressions. On the other hand, systems like Microcosm and CREO made use of large scale corpora to automatically annotate the web page that the user is currently viewing. While Microcosm was keyword based, CREO's corpera instead used two semantic knowledge bases: ConceptNet that derived from human entered common-sense facts (Liu and Singh, 2004) and Stanford TAP that derived from text mining of web crawls (Guha and McCool, 2003). It was thus able to detect key phrases in web pages by textual lookup in the knowledge bases but also know what the phrase means because of the semantic nature of the corpora, for example, knowing that "dog" is a kind of "pet."

Snip!t is also web-page based, but instead of annotating every page, it only looks for actionable terms in areas the user selects to be of interest. For example, Figure 4.21 shows Snip!t recognising potential actions based on a postal code the user has selected. In this respect, it is similar to the early suggestions for the extension of Microcosm to the web (Carr et al., 1994). However, Snip!t uses a combination of corpora (like Microcosm and CREO) and syntactic rules (like early data detectors) with some terms or codes matched only by one or the other and some using a combination. For example, names are matched not simply by patterns of capitalization, but by first noticing that a word in the text is a potential given or family name by matching against large tables of census data and only when such matches are found looking at the broader context to recover the full name.

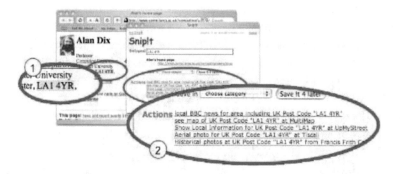

Figure 4.21: Snip!t recognising a postal code: (1) the user selects a region of text and presses the Snip!t bookmarklet (2) the text is recognised as a bookmark and relevant web resources identified (from Dix et al., 2006).

While most of the earlier data detectors and Microcosm tightly bundled the pattern/term to be recognised with the action to be performed, onCue, CREO and Snip!t all separate out the recognition phase from the linking of that to action; that is, they first create implicit semantic annotation and then separately match those semantics to action. This use of an intermediate semantic annotation is intrinsically more flexible, allowing new resources to be added and allowing textual material that was designed purely for human reading to be linked to the larger web of data.

4.1.6   WEB DATA OR ALL DATA?

The web challenges traditional notions of both data bases and user interfaces. Data are varied and more voluminous, and interaction is more collaborative and social. However, it is increasingly becoming the fact that web data is not just a different kind of data, it is radically changing the way in which the users perceive and interact with data. Cloud computing means that even conventional databases are web hosted, and it is becoming rare to find applications that are not either becoming web hosted (such as spreadsheets in Google docs), web delivered (such as desktop and iPhone widgets), or tied to the web (such as help and update systems in virtually every application). So we cannot ignore the web as a place to interact with data.

However, the web confuses many of the boundaries of traditional data management. The semantic web pushes data management towards more formal and explicit semantics, whereas folksonomies encourage more informal and implicit meaning. Yet under it all are often plain old relational databases. The coming years will be an interesting time to see whether the semantic or the social will 'win' or whether they can come together to make something more.

Whatever befalls, the data we have available is vastly greater than in traditional corporate databases, but it is less controlled; as we design applications and interfaces for this, we have many opportunities, but we may have to learn to live with a level of uncertainty.

4.2   MOBILE INTERFACES

Similar to data that do not reside anymore only in databases, user interfaces do not sit anymore on a desk, and sometimes they do not stay in a computer but rather in a cellphone or a PDA: they go mobile. The benefit brought about by mobile computing is unquestionable. Nonetheless, mobile computing has also raised many challenges to both the research and the industrial communities. In particular, we note that the Human–Computer Interaction has yet to fully explore the ramifications of mobile computing. HCI experts have to carefully consider how to make the conventional methods and techniques for the entire design process appropriate to mobile computing. There is a need to have design tools that the designer can use to model user interfaces that are adapted to the characteristics of the context (e.g., the destination device/channel such as PDA, cellphone, etc). Moreover, there is the need to ensure that the realized user interfaces are assessed and refined accordingly (in an iterative manner) toward ensuring that they are inline with the user requirements in the contextual setting (such as mobile settings). As far as mobile interfaces are concerned, we start by discussing the limitations posed by and opportunities presented by mobile computing. We then discuss aspects pertaining to the design and evaluation for usability of mobile user interfaces.

4.2.1   CHALLENGES AND OPPORTUNITIES OF MOBILE COMPUTING

Mobile devices inherently have various limitations including: small screen, limited input modalities, limited computational resources; and wide heterogeneity of operating systems and physical properties. Mobile computing also faces some additional issues, arising from context and interaction as described below:

Variable Context – Since mobile devices, by definition, are mobile, the context in which they are used is continuously changing. This poses challenging new issues because, even if context has always been considered a fundamental aspect to consider and analyze in usability studies, we have only now started to assist to such a frequent and complex variation of it within the same device, application, or single user. A direct implication of this is that designers should find a way to anticipate the conditions in which interaction will happen. This means discovering potential usability flaws that become evident only when considering a user operating in a specific context.

Kind of Interaction – The nature of interaction also changes in mobile settings. In general, users tend to interact in small and focused chunks of activities, more than in fixed settings. A large fraction of tasks in mobile environment consists of few quick steps that the user should be able to execute without cognitive effort. Cognitive effort is the amount of cognitive resources - including perception, memory, and judgment - needed to complete a task (Russo and Dosher, 1983). In addition, mobile tasks may happen in conditions where users' attention is necessarily reduced (for instance, users cannot easily read the screen while walking) or may be part of more complex activities which the conditions should not interfere with.

Interruptions – Mobile devices/applications are always with us. Computation and data can therefore be always available. Notifications and requests for attention should happen in appropriate moments and, in general, some tasks may be interrupted. This raises two kinds of problems: appropriateness of notifications and recovery from interruptions. Applications should find right moments and right ways to advise users, taking into account relevance of notification and user activity. This is important if we consider that context aware systems are mainly based on interaction paradigm where applications can behave proactively, explicitly requesting attention of the user. In addition, we cannot assume that interruptions will not happen, especially in mobile settings where they are even more likely to come. Therefore, designers should find effective strategies to let users smoothly recover from interruptions.

Privacy and Security – Privacy issues become more prominent. While staying mobile, users find themselves in a variety of spaces (e.g., private and public), in a variety of situations (e.g., formal and informal), and in a variety of infrastructures (wireless and cable connection). Moving through these means having different needs for what concerns privacy and security. These must be considered and addressed both by device and application designers, assuring that information is kept secure from intruders.

Intimacy and Availability – Because mobile devices are mobile, they are personally available in a way that fixed devices are not. Moreover, they seem to engender a sense of being "personal" in a deeper sense than fixed devices (e.g., not my PC but *my* PDA and definitely *my* phone). This implies that users depend more on their computing systems than in the past; therefore, their unavailability can create problems that are more serious and intrusive.

It is, however, worth noting that mobile devices present new opportunities in the field of information technologies and in society. They tend to blend, challenge, and sometimes even break conventional human-computer interaction paradigms.

Ubiquitous Access – While being mobile, the user can communicate or be able to use/access remote services/applications and documents. Rather than being tied to fixed settings, the user can operate in multiple and diverse contexts. In a more general sense, mobile devices are instrumental in facilitating the exploitation of the context/environment of the user and the consideration of non-conventional interaction paradigms such as gesture-based and speech-based interactions.

Portability – Mobile devices are generally portable. Their size and weight render them easy to carry along, to move around with and to organize in space.

More Personal than Personal Computer – There tends to be a rather more personal significance that a user attaches to his/her mobile device than to the conventional computing machines/devices such as the desktop computer.

Democratization of Information Access – Through mobile devices, information systems are no longer just limited to experts in information technology/computer science, white-color workers or office personnel. Mobile computing breaks barriers that have limited information systems to a particular type of professionals or workers. It is interesting to observe that there are many opportunities to use information appliances in both formal and informal environments (e.g., for doctors, mechanics, travelers).

Opportunistic Interaction – Access to application and network is allowed *where* it is needed and *when* it is needed. This is probably one of the biggest advantages of mobile devices. Mobile devices represent a powerful resource for mobile users, opening the space for the design of new and challenging applications and services.

Reduced Complexity – While it is true that small screen and limited interaction capabilities extremely reduce the amount of accessible information and the complexity of operations, we can also see this as a benefit. If, in fact, that number of operations and the amount of accessible data are reduced, this means that the overall complexity of the system decreases as well. Because of this, mobile systems may be easier to explore, easier to use, and easier to learn.

4.2.2   USABILITY AND MOBILE COMPUTING

In the following, we discuss challenges encountered in the design and evaluation for usability in mobile computing. The discussion also includes some ways that are being used or that can be used to address such challenges.

Design Challenges and Considerations in Mobile Computing

It is worth noting that the user of a mobile device often has to focus on more than one task because he/she might have to interact with the device (which in itself is a task) while performing the primary task. On the one hand, interaction with the mobile device/application requires, to some extent, user's innate resources (such as attention). On the other hand, the primary task does often require, to an even higher degree, the user's physical, visual and cognitive involvement/resources (such as hands, visual attention, mental focus). The user's physical, visual and cognitive involvement/resources are therefore likely to get constrained. Ideally, the mobile application (including interactions with the device/the non-primary tasks) should support the user in carrying out the primary task rather than "support the user in tampering" with the primary task. We should minimize distracting the user from the primary task or disrupting the user's primary task, unless the disruption/distraction is of genuine (and great) value or of critical importance. In adopting ways to meet the requirement, it is also critical to consider the status of a user's attention in the timing of the tasks on the mobile device (i.e., non-primary tasks). It might be worth counting the costs and gains of deferring an operation/activity to another time when that operation/activity will be less of a distraction. Where necessary, the mobile application should enable/allow the user to temporary halt a task on the device and to resume the interrupted task.

One of the challenges with new or innovative technology/application is that its users may try to use it in situations or ways the designers and developers had never thought of. This is no less true in mobile computing. There is, therefore, a sense in which the user may perform tasks on the device in unpredictable and opportunistic ways. Taking care of all possible use scenarios for a product is a non-trivial challenge for the mobile application analysts and designers. It is also worth observing that the variability of the environment/natural setting may affect the course of a task. Therefore, analysts and designers may also need to account for such variability in the task analysis.

The Model Human Processor model (Card et al., 1983) has been a benchmark for a lot of work in HCI. The model is a simplified view of human processing while interacting with computers. It focuses on the internal cognition driven by the cooperation of: the perceptual system, the motor system, and the cognitive system. Each of the systems maintains its own processing and memory. However, as the role and domain of the computers (and devices) have widened, researchers and designers have been considering models that take into account the relationship between the internal cognition and the outside world (Dix et al., 2004). Some researchers are exploring the following three main models of cognition for possible application in mobile computing: activity theory model, situated action model, and distributed cognition model (Abowd, Mynatt, and Rodden, 2002). The activity theory model is built on concepts such as goals, actions, and operations. Goals and operations are flexible depending on the dynamic nature of the outside world. Moreover, an operation can shift to an action due to a changing situation/context. The model also supports the recognition/acknowledgement of the transformational properties of artifacts. The situated action model allows knowledge in the outside world to constantly mould the ongoing interpretation and execution of a task. The distributed cognition model views the user (internal cognition) as only a part of much larger system. It was observed earlier that tasks on the mobile device (and elsewhere) do sometimes tend to be unpredictable and opportunistic. It is interesting to note that the foregoing models of activity theory, situated action, and distributed cognition could be resourceful in this respect. It is also worth acknowledging the appropriateness of design methods that actively involve the users and observation of users' activities in authentic everyday settings in contributing to design in innovative areas such as ubiquitous computing (Rogers et al., 2002; Strömberg et al., 2004).

Evaluation Challenges and Considerations in Mobile Computing

Conventional user-centered methods could be appropriately exploited in the development of mobile applications. On the same note, some of the traditional usability evaluation techniques might become useful when adapted for mobile computing (Bertini et al., 2006). There are also efforts toward realizing usability principles and heuristics for the design and evaluation of other types of ubiquitous environments/systems, e.g., ambient heuristics (Mankoff et al., 2003) and groupware heuristics (Baker, Greenberg, and Gutwin, 2001).

Much of our understanding about work has its roots in Fordist and Taylorist models of human activity, which assume that human behavior can be decomposed into structured tasks. HCI has not been spared from this either. In particular, evaluation methods in HCI have often relied on measures of task performance and task efficiency as a means of evaluating the underlying application. However, it is not clear whether such measures can be universally applicable when we consider the current move from rather structured tasks (such as desktop activities) and relatively predictable settings to the often unpredictable ubiquitous settings. Such primarily task-centric evaluation may, therefore, not be directly applicable to the mobile computing domain. It would be interesting to consider investigating methods that go beyond the traditional task-centric approaches (Abowd and Mynatt, 2000).

In this era of ubiquitous computing, the real need to take into account the real-world context has become more crucial than at any other time in the history of computing. Although the concept of context is not new to the field of usability (e.g., ISO 9241 guidelines do propose a "model" consideration of context), evaluation methods have however found it challenging, in practice, to adequately/completely integrate the entire context during the evaluation process. Toward addressing the challenge, there are various possibilities. One option is the employment of techniques from other fields that can gain a richer understanding; for instance: ethnography, cultural probes, and contextual inquiry (Dix et al., 2004). Ethnographical methods concentrate on the everyday and routine/common aspects. Cultural probes are intended to uncover the emotional, uncommon and spiritual. Although contextual inquiry resembles ethnographical methods in that it studies the user in context, it differs from ethnographical approaches in that its "intention is to understand and to interpret the data gathered with the explicit aim of designing a new system" (Dix et al., 2004). Ethnographical methods tend to be open ended. It is worth observing, if not emphasizing, that such techniques for gaining a richer understanding of the context can inform both the design and evaluation of mobile applications. Another possibility is to use a 'Wizard-of-Oz' technique or even other simulation techniques such as virtual reality. Such methods are especially appropriate where the mobile application is not fully complete. However, the simulation should closely reflect the real context as much as possible (realistic simulation). Another possibility is by using video data to demonstrate the typical interactions taking place in the real world context as a way to support imagination and immersion in the real setting. For example, video data have been used to support an expert-based evaluation of an e-learning course that was delivered on a mobile device (Gabrielli et al., 2005).

In the formative stages of the design process, low fidelity prototypes, i.e., prototypes with a low degree of functionality and narrow breadth of features, can be used. However, as the design progresses, user tests need to be introduced. In the context of mobile computing, user tests will not only require the inclusion of real users, real setting, and device interaction tasks, but also real or primary tasks (or realistic simulations of the real tasks and of the real settings). As mentioned previously, realistic simulations of the real tasks and of the real settings could be adopted as an alternative. There would, therefore, be the need to provide a prototype that supports the real tasks and real settings, or their simulations. This does imply some cost in the design process because the prototype at this level would need to be sufficiently robust and reliable in order to support primary tasks in real settings or the simulations. In fact, the technology required to develop mobile computing systems is often on the cutting edge. Finding people with cutting edge skills in mobile development is difficult. As a result, developing a reliable and robust mobile computing prototype or application is not easy (Abowd and Mynatt, 2000; Abowd, Mynatt, and Rodden, 2002). Moreover, researchers are deploying mobile devices into various real world settings, e.g., libraries, museums, etc. They are setting up "living laboratories" by creating test beds for advanced research and development in mobile computing (Abowd, Mynatt, and Rodden, 2002).

In summary, mobile and ubiquitous interfaces offer novel opportunities for information access. However, more research is still needed, ranging from new visualizations to diverse validation methods, to make them really effective and usable.

CHAPTER 5

Non-Visual Interfaces

Usability and visual interfaces are key issues, but, if we want to enlarge the user categories that data management systems are addressing, we must broaden the user-centered approach described so far, moving towards the so called *universal access* or *universal usability*.

Universal access refers to the requirement of coping with diversity in: (1) the characteristics of the target user population (including people with disabilities); (2) the scope and nature of tasks; and (3) the different contexts of use (Stephanidis and Savidis, 2001). Shneiderman instead proposes "universal usability" as a term to encompass both accessibility and usability, but notes that "access is not sufficient to ensure successful usage" (Shneiderman, B., 2000). He defines a different ranking of accessibility in comparison to usability: accessibility is a first but not sufficient requirement to achieve universal usability.

5.1 ACCESSIBILITY

The accessibility issue for visual interfaces is gaining increasing interest, mainly driven by web diffusion, and several research activities deal with standards and methodologies for enforcing it (see, e.g., the Web Content Accessibility Guidelines (WCAG, 2008)).

Accessibility is an increasingly relevant concern for data access as well because the accommodation of the needs of the user with various disabilities is a definite requirement, especially when data are the result of a public effort. In the following, we focus on a particular kind of disability: visually-impaired users, because they impose a serious reflection on the way a visual user interfaces are designed. In fact, whilst character-based interfaces offer blind people the extraordinary possibility to make use of their skills in using keyboards and interacting with software tools, graphic interfaces are difficult to manage in an oral interaction. Visual interfaces, in fact, usually imply complex page layouts, many visual features and, above all, the use of the mouse has made their use a difficult and cumbersome task.

Visually-impaired people currently access visual interfaces (e.g., web interfaces) using screen readers, that is, software tools capable of interpreting the HTML code and reading it aloud (with a synthesized voice); interaction is allowed by the use of Braille keyboards or through a combination of key-strokes on the traditional keyboards. The worth of screen readers is clear; nonetheless, their limits are also recognized and discussed in literature (Theofanos and Redish, 2003):

- They read everything, including elements of HTML that are only useful for visualization (and do not convey relevant meaning to the listener).

- They have (by default, at least) a simplistic reading strategy, "top-to-bottom/left-to-right," making it difficult and boring to wait for the relevant piece of information.

- They fail to convey the overall organization of the page, with the relative priorities of the different parts.

- The selection of the navigational commands (e.g., links in a web page) is difficult and cumbersome. While in theory, it is possible to "confirm" the selection while "listening" to a link, in practice; due to synchronization problems (of the audio with the current position on the page), it almost never works.

- Page layout and the "graphic's semantics" (that is, font size and color, position on the page) are completely lost: the metallic voice of the screen reader will read one by one all the pieces of information of the page with the same emphasis and tone (the landmarks, the main content, the service links,…), as if they all shared the same degree of importance.

- Images that convey essential pieces of information are not processed by the screen reader, that is, only able to read an image's description (if available).

The point is that they basically read what appears on the screen, with a "book-reading" strategy, as if it were the most plausible equivalent to the "at a glance" comprehension of a sighted user. The key to finding a proper solution is to separate the *visual* from the *audio* experience: not all that is written or visualized must be read; not all that is read must be visualized on the screen.

A set of accessibility guidelines have been developed (essentially for web interfaces) that may help designers fill the gaps left by current standards (e.g. ,W3C-WAI guidelines) and effectively conceive and deploy applications that are accessible and usable in an *oral navigation*. Innovative design guidelines for supporting "accessible" access paradigms, attempting to go further the limitations of the existing standards are the following:

Navigation strategies: a number of problems for accessibility stems from the practice, for the web and other applications, of forcing the user to "go back" to already visited pages or menu. This practice is ineffective for "normal users" and devastating for blind users (who must go through the whole page before getting to the point of interest). To solve this issue, the designer should be able to communicate the content to the user in a well-structured and understandable way, keeping the displayed text as short as possible. This leads the designers to separate the concept of "topic" from the concept of "page" and to create an application where each topic is made up from different pages, each one related to a point of view or aspect. The main drawback of a structure like the above is that it makes the back button of the browser completely useless in most cases. This button acts as a syntactic back, while what is needed in an information intensive web application is a semantic one, allowing the user to go backward through the topics, instead of browsing all the already visited pages. This is much more important when dealing with accessibility concerns: a visually impaired user has to listen to a significant part of each page to understand what the page is about, even if he/she is going back through her history and knows exactly which page he/she is interested in. Implementing an explicit backward navigation system allows the designer to become more creative: it is possible to provide the content in a different way when the user is coming back to it, to explain it better or to give a quick glance of it. Summarizing:

- The semantic backward navigation should consider only the topics of the website and not all the actual pages of which a topic is made;

- A semantic backward navigation, limiting the intermediate steps needed to reach the desired content, is more comfortable for the user;

- The backward navigation structures and menus have to be well designed. If the designer chooses to provide the content in a different way when the user comes back to it, than it is important that no information is presented that the user did not visit before; otherwise, he/she will not understand why the content he/she is seeing has suddenly changed;

- The back button of the browser should not interfere with the semantic backward navigation: the user should be able to use it without breaking up all the semantic mechanism (this is likely to happen with poorly-designed backward navigation structures when the user goes back - with browser's button – from a topic to the previous one).

Presentation (page) strategies: an oral presentation is radically different from a visual-supported presentation: it is useless to start from the page (from its "look") and to try making it accessible. The goal is, therefore, to develop guidelines for an effective "reading strategy," based upon the intended semantics and the "raw content" of a page, rather than upon its look. A reading strategy can be considered at different levels of granularity: a section, a page, a group of pages, etc.

5.2 AURAL INTERFACES

In this section, we provide an example of an interface for blind people that addresses the guidelines described in the previous section. The example comes from the DELOS NoE project (`http://www.delos.info/`) and is about the Digital Library (ENA), the authoritative multimedia reference to the historical and institutional development of a united Europe from 1945 to the present: more than 15,000 documents of all types (film recordings, sound clips, photos, cartoons, facsimiles, texts, etc.).

ENA is faced with accessibility challenges that often require different or more complex solutions than those that would usually work for the web. As an example, ENA's interface has to work on all screen sizes and be manipulated using a variety of input devices, e.g., the touch-screen terminals do not have a keyboard (traditional or Braille). Some features have been added to improve ENA's overall level of accessibility. The following points are examples of such features:

- Subtitling for a large number of video clips;

- Viewing of video clips in full-screen mode;

Figure 5.1: Screenshots of ENA web site and photo of the multi-touch.

- Option to resize documents whilst retaining optimal display quality;

- Option to zoom in on any element displayed in ENA on the fly (this feature may be activated by selecting a menu option or by turning the scroll wheel whilst holding down the Ctrl key);

- Option to change the interface color scheme to one designed for color-blind users;

- Option to navigate the interface without a pointing device (using the keyboard only).

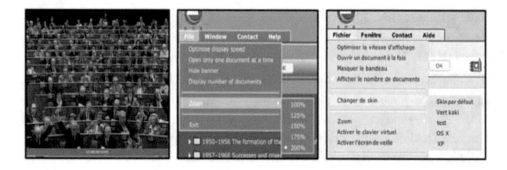

Figure 5.2: Full screen video with subtitles, Zoom capabilities for the whole interface, Skinable interface.

The adaptation of such a digital library for consultation by blind users required more challenging, and sometimes empirical solutions, able to make a screenreader as user-friendly as possible. Unlike traditional web sites, the common element of publication in ENA is not a web page, but a document (text, photo, video, facsimile, map, diagram, etc.) accompanied by structured metadata displayed in a separate window. The prototype is thus based on the same data as the visual version of ENA, but substitutes the point-and-click mode of interaction with listen-and-select. So it is entirely possible that the prototype will be used also by sighted people who prefer this channel of distribution for use in certain situations.

Except for initial development costs, there are no additional maintenance costs, and synchronisation with the visual version is automatic. In this context, the audio version of ENA obviously does not rely on external software, and no screen reader is necessary.

The work undertaken for the development of the prototype has been based mainly on the findings of studies conducted by the DELOS Network of Excellence (http://www.delos.info/). The development of the aural version of ENA requires a preliminary analysis of the types of message (content, interface semantics and navigation) that are exchanged simultaneously with the sighted user.

The ENA interface is designed to give priority to content distribution, given that the content is the library's major asset. Each piece of content is displayed in its own window and is treated as an independent entity throughout: from being stored right through to being displayed.

The various semantic components that the user sees when visiting ENA are made up of the elements that are traditionally found on the Internet (logo, title banner, search field, news and don't miss sections, RSS links) and of elements that are more common to applications (content hierarchy, menu bars, tool bars and language selector).

ENA acts like a desktop application, particularly with regard to the concept of multiple windows. The application acts in a similar way to e-mail clients: there is a hierarchical tree structure in a column on the left and a pane on the right that is split horizontally by a divider, with a synopsis of the subject unit in the preview pane above and a list of documents below (Figure 5.3). It is designed to be intuitive for the average computer user since it draws on the same principles that are applied in the most commonly used operating systems.

The ENA navigation system is relatively simple to use: selecting a topic from the content hierarchy loads a contextual synopsis in the preview pane along with a full list of the multimedia documents available on that particular subject.

Navigation and content in ENA are clearly distinct. Content is displayed in the same way for all subjects and for all documents. The documents do not contain hyperlinks. These features are all unquestionable assets when it comes to adapting ENA for content distribution over a single audio channel.

The new interface prototype has been realized to assess the feasibility of distributing digital library content over an audio channel and to identify the limitations and difficulties linked to the development of an alternative means of consulting ENA visually.

Table 5.1 shows the different kinds of audio streams available in the system that allows for an aural interaction based on the following features:

A brief overview of the application content is available;

Providing the user with an aural 'semantic map' of the entire application; however, this solution only really works effectively where the underlying structure is relatively simple;

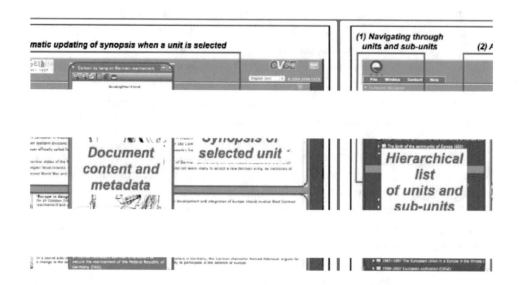

Figure 5.3: Basic navigation principles of ENA.

Providing an executive summary of any list of items (especially long ones);

Defining strategies to partition long lists into smaller, more meaningful chunks;

Providing 'Semantic back' mechanisms emphasising the history of visited pieces of content, rather than the sequence of physical pages;

Providing a semantic navigation mechanism to go 'up' the list of most recently visited items: it is possible to navigate back through the history of documents consulted using the left and right cursor keys;

Keeping consistency across pages by creating aural page templates;

Minimising the number of templates;

Enabling the user to grasp quickly how a page is organised by communicating its structure;

Reading first the key message of the page (e.g., the content) and then the other sections;

Allowing the user to gain direct access to a section of interest at any time.

The audio prototype of ENA is available at http://audio.ena.lu.

Table 5.1: Available audio streams for ENA audio prototype (classified by media types).

Available content for audio publication	ENA documents by media type
ocal synthesis of metadata (caption, keywords, source, opyright) and the entire audio track.	Video clip / Sound clip
ocal synthesis of metadata (caption, keywords, source, opyright) and whole textual content.	Text / Press article / Treaty / Letter / Expert contribution

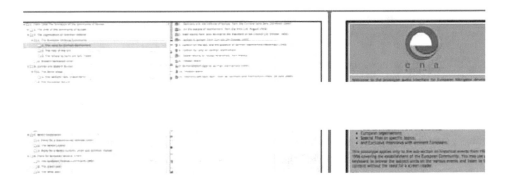

Figure 5.4: ENA audio prototype screenshots (presentation page and main interface).

The right-hand image of Figure 5.4 shows a screenshot of the Flash interface used to gain access to the audio content. Sighted users who are able to use a mouse (and receive visual feedback) should close their eyes and use the keyboard when testing the prototype.

Figure 5.5 shows a comparative graphical representation of navigating ENA visually and aurally. The right diagram might look much more complex on paper than the left one, but after using the audio interface for a while, it is quite surprising how easy it is to use after only a minimal amount of training.

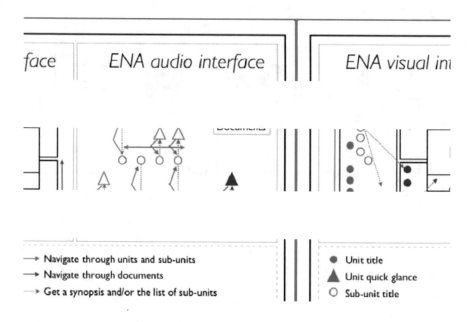

Figure 5.5: Visual browsing versus aural browsing.

The diagram also shows the increased need for user interaction when using the audio interface: unlike in the visual interface, it is not possible to coordinate the distribution of multiple pieces of information simultaneously in the audio interface. The user has to be given the means to control intuitively (with minimal cognitive load) the sequence of the linear flow of information.

CHAPTER 6

Conclusions

A productive interaction between the software system and the user who utilizes it should be a crucial issue in any interactive software. As we noted at the beginning of this lecture, with databases, the needs of the underlying technology often appear most demanding: choosing appropriate data formats, schema, perhaps importing data from heterogeneous sources into consistent relational databases. The user interface can become an afterthought, or worse, users can be seen as an inconvenience, people who may enter incorrect or inconsistent data and, therefore, should be protected against. In recent years, there is evidence that this mentality is changing and the user is gaining the right importance, even if this is happening more slowly than was expected or hoped. One of the keys to ensuring that the user is gaining the right importance is to follow a user-centered approach in designing database systems, putting people at the heart of design. Throughout this lecture, we have seen ways in which effective user-centred design goes beyond simply "putting a nice user interface" on the system. Designing for people must permeate every aspect of the design of a system, from data structures to menu choice. The underlying database can satisfy all the right normalization rules, maintain business logic, or even have an explicit and verified ontology, but if it is not fit for purpose, fit for ultimate use, it is useless.

Along with applying user-centered design techniques, interaction modalities that are more user-oriented than traditional SQL-based interfaces have been proposed and (some of them) tested to prove their usability with real users. Quite a lot of research has concentrated on visual query systems (a good starting point is Zloof's paper on QBE, which dates back to 1977 (Zloof, M., 1977)) and has produced a large number of prototypes and a few commercial softwares. Unfortunately, the impact of such systems has been much less than originally expected. A major step forward in visual query systems may be expected through their interleaving with information visualization techniques. Indeed, there would be no benefit of smart query formulation if coupled with poor result visualization. Information visualization has bloomed tremendously over the last decade, both as a research field and in practical applications. It offers, for instance, an excellent support for interactive data mining or, even simply, information retrieval. Considering that the wealth of information that is available today tends to move the data access issue from database technology to information retrieval technology, information visualization certainly has a bright future.

Visual query systems used to mainly deal with traditional databases, i.e., databases containing alphanumeric data. However, in recent years, the application realms of databases have expanded substantially in terms of both number and variety of data types. As a consequence, specialized systems have been proposed for accessing such new kinds of databases, containing non-conventional data, such as images, videos, maps, etc. Furthermore, the idea of an information repository has been deeply influenced by the beginning of the web age. Different visual systems have been proposed to cope with the need for extracting information residing on the web, though they are not yet satisfactory. In this lecture, the web and mobile interaction have been included as 'advanced applications,' but, in fact, for many in the world, including large parts of Africa, India and China, the only interaction with computation is through web access over a mobile phone. While the desktop-based multi-mega-pixel display visualisation system may be the norm for certain forms of highly expert data analysis, for many users and many applications completely different paradigms will be needed.

More research is needed, in terms not only of different interaction metaphors and modalities, but also of radically different approaches enabling users to focus on the tasks they wish to perform rather than managing information. Making tasks simple for the user requires both intuitive interfaces and sophisticated infrastructure, based on semantic techniques for transparent, automatic but auditable management of data. Moving to task-oriented systems represents a crucial shift from data-centric user interfaces, which have characterized over forty years of Computer Science. Furthermore, user interfaces need to be able to interpret the user's aims and to support context dependent execution of the user's tasks.

Finally, while desktop visual interfaces and information visualization techniques (often with large displays) are usually considered the most usable approaches, they assume unimpaired vision and cognitive abilities, not to mention often a level of technical sophistication. There are many, the disabled, the elderly, the very young, for whom these assumptions do not apply. Furthermore, even for the fully-abled and well-trained users, there are circumstances, such as heavy stress and poor working conditions. For these, users and/or contexts existing complex visual interfaces may not be appropriate, so other interactive paradigms need to be explored offering interaction choices, which allow equivalent functionality but fits the user's needs and preferences.

Bibliography

G. D. Abowd and E. D. Mynatt Charting Past, Present, and Future Research in Ubiquitous Computing. *ACM Transactions on Computer-Human Interaction*, 7(1):29–58, 2000. DOI: 10.1145/344949.344988 73, 74

G. D. Abowd, E. D. Mynatt, and T. Rodden The Human Experience. *IEEE Pervasive Computing*, 2(2):48–57, 2002. DOI: 10.1109/MPRV.2002.993144 72, 74

C. Ahlberg and B. Shneiderman Visual Information Seeking: Tight Coupling of Dynamic Query Filters with Starfield Displays. In *Proc. ACM Conference on Human Factors in Computing Systems (SIGCHI)*, pages 313–317, 1994. DOI: 10.1145/191666.191775 17

M. Angelaccio, T. Catarci, and G. Santucci QBD*: A Graphical Query Language with Recursion. *IEEE Trans. Software Eng.*, 16(10):1150–1163, 1990. DOI: 10.1109/32.60295 17

P. André, M. L. Wilson, A. Russell, D. A. Smith, A. Owens, and M. C. Schraefel Continuum: Designing timelines for hierarchies, relationships and scale. In *Proc. ACM Symposium on User Interface Software and Technology*, 2007. DOI: 10.1145/1294211.1294229 42, 62

M. Ankerst *Visual Data Mining*. PhD thesis, University of Munich, 2000. 41, 42

M. Ankerst Visual Data Mining with Pixel-oriented Visualization Techniques. In *Proc. KDD Workshop on Visual Data Mining*, 2001. 41

K. Baker, S. Greenberg, and C. Gutwin Heuristic Evaluation of Groupware Based on the Mechanics of Collaboration. In *Proc. 8th IFIP Working Conference on Engineering for Human-Computer Interaction (EHCI'01)*, 2001. 73

D. Barbar, W. DuMouchel, C. Faloutsos, P. J. Haas, J. M. Hellerstein, Y. E. Ioannidis, H. V. Jagadish, T. Johnson, R. T. Ng, V. Poosala, K. A. Ross, and K. C. Sevcik The New Jersey data reduction report. *IEEE Data Eng. Bull.*, 20(4):3–45, 1997. 24

M. Bergman and F. Giasson zLinks: Semantic Framework for Invoking Contextual Linked Data. In *Proc. Linked Data on the Web (LDOW2008)*, 2008. 66

T. Berners-Lee Weaving the Web: The Original Design and Ultimate Destiny of the World Wide Web by its Inventor. HarperOne, 1999. 49

T. Berners-Lee, Y. Chen, L. Chilton, D. Connolly, R. Dhanaraj, J. Hollenbach, A. Lerer, and D. Sheets Tabulator: Exploring and Analyzing linked data on the Semantic Web. In *Proc. 3rd International Semantic Web User Interaction Workshop (SWUI06)*, 2006. 60

T. Berners-Lee, J. Hendler, and O. Lassila The Semantic Web. *Scientific American Magazine*, 2001. DOI: 10.1038/scientificamerican0501-34 50

J. Bertin *Graphics and Graphic Information Processing*. Walter de Gruyter & Co., Berlin, 1981. 18

E. Bertini, T. Catarci, A. Dix, S. Gabrielli, S. Kimani, and G. Santucci Appropriating Heuristic Evaluation Methods for Mobile Computing. *Int. J. of Mobile Human Computer Interaction*, 1(1):20–41, 2009. 4

E. Bertini, S. Gabrielli, S. Kimani, T. Catarci, and G. Santucci Appropriating and Assessing Heuristics for Mobile Computing. In *Proc. Advanced Visual Interfaces (AVI)*, 2006. DOI: 10.1145/1133265.1133291 73

E. Bertini and G. Santucci Give chance a chance: modeling density to enhance scatter plot quality through random data sampling. *Information Visualization*, 5(2):95–110, 2006. DOI: 10.1057/palgrave.ivs.9500122 35

R. Bias and D. Mayhew *Cost-Justifying Usability*. Second Edition. Morgan Kaufmann, 2005. 5

C. Bizer, T. Heath, and T. Berners-Lee Linked Data – The Story So Far. *Int. J. on Semantic Web and Information Systems*, 5(3):1–22, 2009. 12, 58

J. Boulos, N. Dalvi, B. Mandhani, S. Mathur, C. Re, and D. Suciu Mystiq: a system for finding more answers by using probabilities. In *Proc. ACM SIGMOD international conference on Management of data*, pages 891–893, ACM Press, 2005. DOI: 10.1145/1066157.1066277 23

D. Brickley and L. Miller An Introduction to RDFWeb and FOAF. Originally at `http://rdfweb.org/2000/08/why/`, Now at `http://www.foaf-project.org/original-intro`, 2000. 51

D. Calvanese, G. De Giacomo, D. Lembo, M. Lenzerini, and R. Rosati Conceptual modeling for data integration. In A. Borgida, V. K. Chaudhri, P. Giorgini, and E. S. K. Yu, editors, *Conceptual Modeling: Foundations and Applications (Lecture Notes in Computer Science)*, 5600:173–197, Springer, 2009. DOI: 10.1007/978-3-642-02463-4 22

S. K. Card, J. D. Mackinlay, and B. Shneiderman *Readings in Information Visualization*. Morgan Kaufmann, 1999. 11, 41

S. K. Card, T. P. Moran, and A. Newell *The Psychology of Human-Computer Interaction*. Lawrence Erlbaum Associates, 1983. 72

L. A. Carr, W. Hall, H. C. Davis, D. C. DeRoure, and R. Hollom The Microcosm Link Service and its Application to the World Wide Web. In *Proc. World Wide Web Conference*, 1994. 68

T. Catarci, M. F. Costabile, S. Levialdi, and C. Batini Visual Query Systems for Databases: A Survey. *J. Visual Languages and Computing*, 8(2):215–260, 1997. DOI: 10.1006/jvlc.1997.0037 9

T. Catarci, A. J. Dix, A. Katifori, G. Lepouras, and A. Poggi Task-Centred Information Management. In *Proc. DELOS Conference*, pages 197–206, 2007. 12

T. Catarci and G. Santucci The Prototype of the DARE System. In *Proc. ACM Int. Conf. on Management of Data* 609, 2001. DOI: 10.1145/376284.375771 12

T. Catarci, G. Santucci, and S. F. Silva An Interactive Visual Exploration of Medical data for Evaluating Health Centres. *Journal of Research and Practice in Information Technology*, 35(2):99–119, 2003. 12

E. F. Codd, S. B. Codd, and C. T. Salley Providing olap (on-line analytical processing) to user-analysis. *An IT Mandate*, 1993. 24

K. G. Cox, S. G. Eick, G. J. Wills, and R. J. Brachman Visual Data Mining: Recognizing Telephone Calling Fraud. *Knowledge Discovery and Data Mining*, 1(2):225–231, 1997. DOI: 10.1023/A:1009740009307 44

T. F. Cox and M. A. A. Cox *Multidimensional Scaling*. Chapman & Hall, 1994. 24

I. F. Cruz, K. M. James, and D. C. Brown Integrating Layout in Multimedia Information Retrieval. In *Proc. AAAI Fall Symposium on Using Layout for the Generation, Understanding or Retrieval of Documents*, 1999. 12

A. Dix Tasks = Data + Action + Context: Automated Task Assistance through Data-Oriented Analysis. In *Proc. 2nd Conference on Human-Centered Software Engineering and 7th international Workshop on Task Models and Diagrams*, 2008. DOI: 10.1007/978-3-540-85992-5_1 68

A. Dix, R. Beale, and A. Wood Architectures to make Simple Visualisations using Simple Systems. In *Proc. Advanced Visual Interfaces (AVI 2000)*, pages 51–60, ACM Press, 2000. DOI: 10.1145/345513.345250 67

A. Dix, T. Catarci, B. Habegger, Y. Ioannidis, A. Kamaruddin, A. Katifori, G. Lepouras, A. Poggi, and D. Ramduny-Ellis Intelligent context-sensitive interactions on desktop and the web. In *Proc. International Workshop on Context in Advanced interfaces (in conjunction with AVI 2006)*, 2006. DOI: 10.1145/1145706.1145710 68

A. Dix, J. Finlay, G. Abowd, and R. Beale *Human-Computer Interaction*. Third Edition, Prentice Hall, 2004. 1, 72, 73

S. G. Eick Visualizing multidimensional data. *SIGGRAPH Comput. Graph*, 34(1):61–67, 2000. DOI: 10.1145/563788.604454 24

G. Ellis and A. Dix A taxonomy of clutter reduction for information visualization. *IEEE Visualization*, 2007. DOI: 10.1109/TVCG.2007.70535 35

A. Elmagarmid, P. Ipeirotis, and V. Verykios Duplicate record detection: A survey. *IEEE Transactions on Knowledge and Data Engineering*, 19(1):1–16, 2007. DOI: 10.1109/TKDE.2007.250581 23

A. Faaborg and H. Lieberman A Goal-Oriented Web Browser. In *Proc. ACM Conference on Human Factors in Computing Systems (SIGCHI)*, pages 751–760, ACM Press, 2006. DOI: 10.1145/1124772.1124883 68

U. Fayyad, G. Piatetsky-Shapiro, and P. Smyth Knowledge Discovery and Data Mining: Towards a Unifying Framework. In *Proc. International Conference on Knowledge Discovery and Data Mining*, 1996. 40

U. Fayyad, G. Piatetsky-Shapiro, P. Smyth, and R. Uthurusamy *Advances in Knowledge Discovery and Data Mining*. AAAI Press/MIT Press, 1996. 40

R. T. Fielding Architectural Styles and the Design of Network-based Software Architectures. PhD thesis, University of California, Irvine, 2000. 51, 61

P. Forbrig and F. Paternò *Lecture Notes in Computer Science*, 5247:1–13 Springer-Verlag, Berlin, Heidelberg, 2008.

S. Gabrielli, V. Mirabella, S. Kimani, and T. Catarci Supporting Cognitive Walkthrough with Video Data: A Mobile Learning Evaluation Study. In *Proc. Mobile HCI 05*, 2005. DOI: 10.1145/1085777.1085791 74

M. Ganesh, E. H. Han, V. Kumar, S. Shekhar, and J. Srivastava *Visual Data Mining: Framework and Algorithm Development*. Tech. Rep. TR-96–021, University of Minnesota, 1996. 41, 42

D. Goodman *Dynamic HTML: The Definitive Reference*. Third Edition, O'Reilly Media, 2006. 50

J. Greenbaum and M. Kyng *Design at Work: Cooperative Design of Computer Systems*. Lawrence Erlbaum, 1991. 3

M. Gross Visual Computing: The Integration of Computer Graphics, Visual Perception and Imaging. Springer-Verlag, 1994. 41

R. Guha and R. McCool TAP: a Semantic Web Platform. Computer Networks. *The International Journal of Computer and Telecommunications Networking*, 42(5), 2003. DOI: 10.1016/S1389-1286(03)00225-1 68

E. M. Haber, Y. Ioannidis, and M. Livny Foundations of visual metaphors for schema display. *Journal of Intelligent Information Systems*, 3(3/4):263–298, 1994. DOI: 10.1007/BF00962239 11, 12

W. Hall, H. Davis, and G. Hutchings *Rethinking Hypermedia: The Microcosm Approach*. Kluwer Academic Publishers, 1996. 67

J. Han, Y. Fu, W. Wang, J. Chiang, W. Gong, K. Koperski, D. Li, Y. Lu, A. Rajan, N. Stefanovic, B. Xia, and O. R. Zaiane DBMiner: A System for Mining Knowledge in Large Relational Databases. In *Proc. International Conference on Knowledge Discovery and Data Mining*, 1996. 45

M. Hao, U. Dayal, M. Hsu, J. Becker, and R. D'Eletto *A Java-Based Visual Mining Infrastructure and Applications*. Tech. Rep. HPL-1999–49, HP Labs, 1999. 45

M. Hao, U. Dayal, M. Hsu, R. D'Eletto, and J. Becker A Java-Based Visual Mining Infrastructure and Applications. In *Proc. IEEE International Symposium on Information Visualization*, pages 124–127, IEEE Computer Society Press, 1999. DOI: 10.1109/INFVIS.1999.801867 45

D. Harel On Visual Formalism. *Communications of the ACM*, 31(5):514–530, 1988. DOI: 10.1145/42411.42414 11, 58

T. Heath Linked Data - Connect Distributed Data across the Web. linkeddata.org, 2008. 58

A. Holdener *Ajax: The Definitive Guide*. O'Reilly Media, 2008. 50

A. Inselberg and B. Dimsdale The plain with parallel coordinate, special issue on computational geometry. *The Visual Computer*, 1:69–97, 1985. DOI: 10.1007/BF01898350 29

S. Kimani, T. Catarci, and G. Santucci A Visual Data Mining Environment. Visual Data Mining *Lecture Notes in Computer Science*, 331–366, 2008. DOI: 10.1007/978-3-540-71080-6_20 46

T. Kohonem *Self-organizing maps*. Springer, 2001. 24

I. Kopanakis and B. Theodoulidis Visual Data Mining and Modeling Techniques In *Proc. KDD Workshop on Visual Data Mining*, 2001. DOI: 10.1016/j.jvlc.2003.06.002 41, 42, 43

G. Krasner and S. Pope A cookbook for using the model-view-controller user interface paradigm in Smalltalk-80. *JOOP*, 1(3), 1988. 57

H. Liu and P. Singh ConceptNet: a Practical Commonsense Reasoning Toolkit. *BT Technology Journal*, 2004. DOI: 10.1023/B:BTTJ.0000047600.45421.6d 68

J. D. Mackinlay *Automatic Design of Graphical Presentations*. PhD thesis, Department of Computer Science, Stanford University, 1986. 11

J. D. Mackinlay, G. G. Robertson, and S. K. Card The perspective wall: detail and context smoothly integrated. In *Proc. ACM Conference on Human Factors in Computing Systems (SIGCHI)*, ACM Press, 1991. DOI: 10.1145/108844.108870 35

J. Mankoff, A. K. Dey, G. Hsieh, J. Kientz, S. Lederer, and M. Ames Heuristic Evaluation of Ambient Displays. In *Proc. ACM Conference on Human Factors in Computing Systems (SIGCHI)*, pages 169–176, 2003. DOI: 10.1145/642611.642642 73

P. Markopoulos, J. C. Read, S. J. MacFarlane, and J. Hoysniemi *Evaluating Interactive Products with and for Children*. Morgan Kaufmann Publishers, 2008. 3

R. S. Michalski, R. S., Bratko, I. and M. Kubat 1999. *Machine Learning and Data Mining*. John Wiley and Sons. 41

T. Mihalisin and J. Timlin Fast Robust Visual Data Mining. *In Proc. International Conference on Knowledge Discovery and Data Mining*, pages 231–234, AAAI Press, 1995. 46

T. Mihalisin, J. Timlin, and J. Schwegler Visualization and Analysis of Multi-Variate Data: A Technique for All Fields. *In Proc. International Conference on Visualization*, 1991. 46

W. Mitchell Representation. In F. Lentricchia and T. McLaughlin, editors. *Critical Terms for Literary Study*. University of Chicago Press, 1995. 10

L. Mohan and R. L. Kashyap A Visual Query Language for Graphical Interaction With Schema-Intensive Databases. *IEEE Transactions on Knowledge and Data Engineering* 5(5):843–858, 1993. DOI: 10.1109/69.243513 15

B. Nardi, J. Miller, and D. Wright Collaborative, Programmable Intelligent Agents. *Communications of the ACM*, 41(3):96–104, 1998. DOI: 10.1145/272287.272331 67

F. Naumann and M. Herschel *An Introduction to Duplicate Detection*. Morgan & Claypool, 2010. DOI: 10.2200/S00262ED1V01Y201003DTM003 23

T. M. Newcomb *Social Psychology*. London, Tavistock, 1952. 18

J. Nielsen Enhancing the explanatory power of usability heuristics. *In Proc. ACM Conference on Human Factors in Computing Systems (SIGCHI)*, pages 152–158, 1994. DOI: 10.1145/191666.191729 4

J. Nielsen *Ten Usability Heuristics*. http://www.useit.com/papers/heuristic/heuristic_list.html, 2005 (accessed May 1 2010) 4

J. Nielsen and T. Landauer A mathematical model of the finding of usability problems. *In Proc. INTERACT '93 and ACM Conference on Human Factors in Computing Systems (SIGCHI)*, pages 206–213, 1993. DOI: 10.1145/169059.169166 7

G. M. Nielson, H. Hagen, and H. Muller *Scientific Visualization: Overviews, Methodologies, and Techniques*. IEEE Computer Society, 1997. 41

T. O'Reilly *What Is Web 2.0: Design Patterns and Business Models for the Next Generation of Software.* http://oreilly.com/web2/archive/what-is-web-20.html, 2005 (accessed May 1 2010). 49

M. Pandit and S. Kalbag The selection recognition agent: Instant access to relevant information and operations. *In Proc. Intelligent User Interfaces (IUI)*, pages 47–52, ACM Press, 1997. DOI: 10.1145/238218.238285 67

P. Pfaff and P. ten Hagen Seeheim Workshop on User Interface Management Systems. Springer-Verlag, 1985. 57

S. Powers *Practical RDF.* O'Reilly Media, 2003. 57

J. Preece, Y. Rogers, H. Sharp, D. Benyon, S. Holland, and T. Carey *Human Computer Interaction.* Addison Wesley, 1994. 1

R. Rao and S. K. Card The Table Lens: Merging Graphical and Symbolic Representations in an Interactive Focus+Context Visualization for Tabular Information. *In Proc. ACM Conference on Human Factors in Computing Systems (SIGCHI)*, ACM Press, 1994. DOI: 10.1145/259963.260391 35

Y. Rogers, M. Scaife, H. Muller, C. Randell, A. Moss, I. Taylor, E. Harris, H. Smith, S. Price, T. Phelps, G. Corke, S. Gabrielli, D. Stanton, and C. O'Malley Things aren't what they seem to be: innovation through technology inspiration. *In Proc. 4th ACM Conference on Designing interactive Systems (DIS)*, pages 373–378, 2002. DOI: 10.1145/778712.778766 73

J.E. Russo and B. A. Dosher Strategies for Multiattribute Binary Choice. *Journal of Experimental Psychology: Learning, Memory, and Cognition*, 9:676–696, 1983. DOI: 10.1037/0278-7393.9.4.676 70

J. Schneidewind, M. Sips, and D. A. Keim Pixnostics: Towards measuring the value of visualization. *In Proc. IEEE Symposium on Visual Analytics Science and Technology*, pages 199–206, 2006. DOI: 10.1109/VAST.2006.261423 37

D. Schon The Reflective Practitioner: How Professionals Think in Action. Ashgate Publishing, 1991. 3

Y. Shirota, Y. Shirai, and T. L. Kunii Sophisticated Form-Oriented Database Interface for Non-Programmers. *In Proc. Visual Database Systems*, pages 127–155, 1989. 14

B. Shneiderman Universal usability. *Communications of the ACM*, 43(5):85–91, 2000. DOI: 10.1145/332833.332843 75

B. Shneiderman, C. Plaisant, M. Cohen, and S. Jacobs *Designing the User Interface: Strategies for Effective Human-Computer Interaction.* 5th Edition. Addison Wesley, 2009. 1

S. J. Simoff Towards the Development of Environments for Designing Visualisation Support for Visual Data Mining. *In Proc. ECML/PKDD Workshop on Visual Data Mining*, 2001. 41, 48

I. Sommerville *Software Engineering*. 7th Edition. Addison Wesley, 2004. 6

R. Spence *Information Visualization: Design for Interaction*. 2nd Edition. Pearson/Prentice hall, 2007. 26, 30

C. Stephanidis and A. Savidis Universal Access in the Information Society: Methods, Tools and Interaction Technologies. *Universal Access in the Information Society Journal*, 40–55, Springer-Verlag, 2001. 75

H. Strömberg, V. Pirttilä, and V. Ikonen Interactive scenarios-building ubiquitous computing concepts in the spirit of participatory design. *Personal and Ubiquitous Computing*, 8:200–207, 2004. DOI: 10.1007/s00779-004-0278-7 73

J. Stylos, B. Myers, and A. Faulring Citrine: providing intelligent copy-and-paste. *In Proc. 17th Symposium on User Interface Software and Technology*, pages 185–188, ACM Press, 2004. DOI: 10.1145/1029632.1029665 68

M. F. Theofanos and J. D. Redish Guidelines for Accessible – and Usable – Web Sites: Observing Users Who Work With Screenreaders. *Interactions*, x(6):36–51, 2003. 75

K. Tsuda, A. Yoshitaka, M. Hirakawa, M. Tanaka, and T. Ichikawa Iconic Browser: An Iconic Retrieval System for Object-Oriented Databases. *Journal of Visual Languages and Computing*, 1(1):59–76, 1990. DOI: 10.1016/S1045-926X(05)80034-5 16

E. R. Tufte *The Visual Display of Quantitative Information*. Graphics Press, Cheshire, CO, 1983. 10

E. R. Tufte *Envisioning Information*. Graphics Press, Cheshire, CO, 1990. 10

E. R. Tufte *Visual Explanations*. Cheshire, CT, Graphics Press, 1997. 19

J. W. Tukey *Exploratory Data Analysis*. Addison-Wesley, 1977. 26, 37

W3C Resource Description Framework (RDF). *The World Wide Web Consortium (W3C)*. http://www.w3.org/RDF/, 2010 (accessed May 1 2010). 57

C. Ware Information Visualization – Perception for design. Morgan Kaufmann, 2000. 25, 29

WCAG *Web Content Accessibility Guidelines (WCAG) 2.0*. http://www.w3.org/TR/WCAG20/, 2008 (accessedMay12010). 75

L. Wilkinson, A. Anand, and R. Grossman Graph-theoretic scagnostics. *In Proc. IEEE Symposium on Information Visualization*, pages 157–164, 2005. DOI: 10.1109/INFVIS.2005.1532142 37

G. J. Wills NicheWorks: Interactive Visualization of Very Large Graphs. *In Proc. Symposium on Graph Drawing*, 1997. DOI: 10.1007/3-540-63938-1_85 44

G. J. Wills NicheWorks: Interactive Visualization of Very Large Graphs. *Journal of Computational and Graphical Statistics*, 8(2):190–212, 1999. DOI: 10.2307/1390633 44

A. Wood, A. Dey, and G. Abowd Cyberdesk: Automated Integration of Desktop and Network Services. *In Proc. ACM Conference on Human Factors in Computing Systems (SIGCHI)*, pages 552–553, ACM Press, 1997. DOI: 10.1145/258549.259031 67

M. M. Zloof Query-by-Example: A Database Language. *IBM Syst. Journal* 16(4):324–343, 1977. DOI: 10.1147/sj.164.0324 9, 14, 83

Authors' Biographies

TIZIANA CATARCI

Tiziana Catarci obtained her Ph.D. in Computer Engineering in 1992 from the University of Roma "La Sapienza", Italy, where she is now a full professor. Her main research interests are in theoretical and application oriented aspects of visual formalisms for databases, information visualization, database design, cooperative information systems, user interfaces, usability, digital libraries, data quality and Web access. On these topics, she has published over 150 papers in leading journals and conferences and 20 books. Her contributions can be regarded as one of the first and most significant examples of deep analysis and formalization of the interaction between the user and the database, which takes in consideration both usability issues and language related aspects.

ALAN DIX

Alan Dix is Professor of Computing at Lancaster University. His work in HCI research has spanned 25 years and has included the study of formal methods for interactive systems (his thesis topic), collaborative work, and web and mobile interfaces. His recent work has focused on intelligent Internet interfaces, physicality in design and methods for technical creativity. He has published over 300 technical papers and authored and co-authored several books including one of the main international textbooks in human-computer interaction. In addition to his HCI research, he was involved in two dot.com start-ups, and recently, he was co-inventor of intelligent lighting technology, which is currently under commercial development.

STEPHEN KIMANI

Stephen Kimani is a Research Scientist with CSIRO ICT Centre (Australia). He has been a post-doctoral researcher with the University of Rome "La Sapienza" (Italy). He holds a PhD in Computer Engineering (University of Rome "La Sapienza", Italy, 2004) and MSc in Advanced Computing (University of Bristol, UK, 1998). His main area of research is Human-Computer Interaction (HCI) and in particular usability, user interface design, mobile computing, visual information access, and accessibility. He has published widely and is serving as a member of a Program Committee for several international HCI conferences.

GIUSEPPE SANTUCCI

Giuseppe Santucci is Associate Professor at the Department of Computer Science of Sapienza Università di Roma. His main research activities concern user interfaces to databases, human-computer interaction, and information visualization, focusing on expressive power and topological properties of visual query languages for semantic data models, on user interfaces development and assessment, on evaluation and quality aspects of Information Visualization techniques, on visual analytics, and visual data mining. On such topics he published more than 90 papers in international journals and conferences. He has served in various roles for conferences in the areas of data management and user interfaces, most notably general chair and programme chair of AVI 2010, the ACM conference on advanced visual interfaces.

Printed in the United States
by Baker & Taylor Publisher Services